As Baltek grasps the huge cornerstone, a click echoes out of the murky passageway. You step closer to the gloomy doorway and peer inside. A pitch-black curtain of darkness greets your eyes.

You hear another click, and then another! Finally, dragon skeleton creeps into the dim light. It must measure forty feet from the end of its toothy mouth to the last tiny tailbone. Two wicked horns, nearly as long as Baltek's arms, rise out of its forehead.

"The Guardian of the Cube!" Lydia screams. "We must flee or die!"

"And leave the Cube of Mystic Forces?" Pentegarn gasps. "Never! Without it, our mission is doomed!"

1.) If you choose to stay and battle the gruesome guardian, turn to page 128.

2.) But if you're going to flee the mighty monster, leaving the cube behind, turn to page 52.

The choice is yours. The chance that you can defeat the dragon skeleton is very small, indeed. But if you flee, you may not find another path to victory.

Only you can pick your path to adventure, to fame and fortune, or to disaster!

You Pick Your Own Path to Adventure!

DUNGEONS & DRAGONS™
ENDLESS QUEST™ BOOK
Pick-A-Path to Adventure

PILLARS of PENTEGARN

by Rose Estes

Illustrated by Harry J. Quinn
Cover by Larry Elmore
Editor: Troy Denning
D&D® Consultant: Frank Mentzer

From TSR's Education Department

The Game Wizards

For my father, who believed in me.

Distributed to the book trade in the United States by Random House
    Inc., and in Canada by Random House of Canada, Ltd.,
Distributed in the United Kingdom by TSR Hobbies (UK) Ltd.
Distributed to the toy and hobby trade by regional distributors.

TSR Hobbies, Inc.   TSR Hobbies, Inc.
POB 756   The Mill, Rathmore Road
Lake Geneva, WI 53147   Cambridge CB14AD
                        United Kingdom

ISBN 0-935696-92-X

Second Printing: July 1982
Printed in the United States of America
Library of Congress Catalog Card Number: 82-50560

This book is a DUNGEONS & DRAGONS™ ENDLESS QUEST™ adventure book. Between the cover of this book, you will find many paths to fantasy adventure.

You can read this book many times with many different results, so if you make an unwise choice, go back to the beginning and start again.

There are many possible choices in this story; some simple, some sensible, some foolhardy...some dangerous! You make all the decisions.

scaly, bark-covered hand wraps its long thin fingers around your shoulder. A wispy voice whispers, "Excuse me, friend. I need to tidy up around you."

Your friend Tree lowers a branch and you climb on eagerly. You are always happy to rest in Tree's branches and watch your friends scurry about the forest.

You are Jaimie, a young villager living at the edge of a mysterious forest. Although the people of your village tell tales of woodland terrors and ferocious beasts lurking in these woods, you have spent your happiest moments rambling through the forest, climbing Tree's craggy trunk, and playing with your friends, Fox and Owl.

While Tree's leafy fingers straighten flower stems and brush his knobby roots, you listen to him discuss a party of adventurers with Fox and Owl.

"I thought them an exceptional group," Tree says. "When they built their campfire, they gathered only dead wood. They did not break any of my branches, nor did they carve my bark. When they left, they put out their fire and cleaned their campsite."

"Well, I think they're heading for trouble," says Fox. "I followed them when they left this morning. They went off toward the river, but then they back-tracked and started toward the Pillars of Pentegarn!"

Owl gasps, "The Pillars of Pentegarn! Surely, you are mistaken!"

"No way, birdbrain," Fox snaps. "Do you think I have this nose for nothing? I can track anything, and their little tricks aren't going to fool me. If I say they were going to the Pillars of Pentegarn, that's where they were going!"

There is a long silence. The Pillars of Pentegarn lie in the most frightening part of the forest. Not even the bravest creatures go there.

"Hide!" Tree says suddenly. "Fast! I see goblins coming up the path!"

You jump down and skitter under a bush. Owl flutters high into Tree's branches. Fox hides behind a rock, then changes his mind and runs for the forest. He is in plain sight when the goblins march into the clearing.

Without pausing, the goblins throw their spears at Fox. He yelps and runs into the bushes. The spears miss him, but they thud solidly into Tree, whose breeze-like groans pass unheard by the monsters.

"Missed!" grunts one.

"Doesn't matter. Fox taste bad," answers another.

"Don't care about taste. Hunting is funnest part."

The largest goblin rips its spear out of Tree, then drops to all fours and sniffs the ground. "Girl's scarf," it says, picking up a white kerchief. "They been here. Close now."

The goblins crowd around their leader, pushing and shoving each other. Finally, the largest goblin pushes its way out of the crowd and runs down the trail toward the river. The others follow quickly.

When the last goblin pounds down the path, you scurry out from beneath your bush and rush to Tree. He moans softly and his branches sway in pain.

You inspect the wounds and plug them with wet, clean moss. The flow of sap slowly stops. Tree has calmed, and only an occasional movement of his branches tells you he suffers great pain.

Owl climbs down as soon as you finish patching Tree's trunk. A goblin spear has pierced his left wing. "Do not be overly concerned," gasps Owl. "They just winged me." You remove the spear and carefully press a pad of moss onto the wound.

Fox returns and inspects his wounded friends. "Wow! Can you imagine what they'll do to those adventurers?" he asks.

"I don't want to think about it," you say.

"But you must!" urges Tree. "If we don't warn them, they won't stand a chance. We must do something!"

"Don't look at me, I can't warn them," Fox says. "You're the only human I'm on speaking terms with."

"Fox is correct," Owl says. "You are the only human I have ever met who talks to animals. It would be useless for Fox or myself to attempt to warn the adventurers, for they would not understand us. You must warn them, Jaimie."

1. Warn the adventurers of their danger; turn to page 100.
2. Or return home, deciding you are too frightened to risk meeting the goblins again. Turn to page 9.

"Let Baltek do what he does best—fight!" you say. "Let's go straight to the tower. The longer we sneak around, the more likely we are to get caught."

Pentegarn looks at you sadly for a long moment. You have the dreadful feeling you have disappointed him deeply.

He says, in a tired old-man voice, "Come, gather round me and do exactly as I say."

He turns and taps the wall with his staff. Snick! The wall opens, and cool darkness surrounds you. You realize night has fallen.

You walk onto a narrow ledge battered by fierce winds. The ruins of the kingdom lie on your left. To your right, there is a dizzying fall into a valley thousands of feet below.

Pentegarn looks like a swirling gray cloud as the wind whips his cloak and hair against his frail body.

"Is it too late to go home?" asks Fox.

"Put all thoughts of home from your minds," says Pentegarn, pointing his staff up the mountain. "That is our destination."

In the distance, you see a tall, narrow tower standing against the stormy night sky. A narrow spine of rock connects it to the mountain. One dim light burns at the tower's base.

"We have only one way of getting to the tower safely," says Pentegarn. "Although it has its risks, too."

Please turn to page 12.

Fortunately, you have time to do your chores before your mother returns.

Even though the south wind holds, you do not have any desire to run off to the woods. Over the next few days, you're so good your mother thinks you're sick. But you're not sick, you're just scared.

You often wonder how the adventurers are doing, but since you would need to go to the Pillars of Pentegarn to find out, the question remains unanswered.

Would your help have made any difference?

Unfortunately, you'll never know.

THE END

For another adventure, go back to the beginning and try again.

The goblins are approaching too fast for you to escape.

"Hurry," says Pentegarn, "follow me!"

Pentegarn leads you to a hill overlooking the path and tells you his plan. The ugly jabbering creatures arrive all too soon. They rush along the narrow path below the hill.

On Pentegarn's signal, you all rise and throw slabs of broken rock down upon the unsuspecting goblins. Screams of terror and rage burst forth from the foul monsters. They scramble to escape, but the hill is too steep. You continue to hurl the rubble down upon their heads, burying them all within minutes.

"We have won this encounter," Pentegarn gasps after the last rock is thrown, "But it appears our passage will not pass unnoticed. Quickly, into the cavern!"

You follow Pentegarn into the cavern, and once again you are traveling on a high ledge, this time inside the mountain. Vast numbers of goblins make machines of war on the cavern floor far below.

Never have you seen so many goblins!

All of you stop for a moment, stunned by the terrible sight. As you watch, the goblins at the far end of the cavern begin to mill about in fear. Finally, they abandon order and run in all directions.

A familiar dry clacking noise reaches your ears, and you see the reason for the goblins' panic. A skeleton patrol appears, marching in dreadful deadly precision. It makes you feel better to see the goblins scattering in fear, and you take advantage of their confusion to hurry along the ledge unnoticed.

When you reach the end of the ledge, Pentegarn says, "We have two choices now. We can sneak through the dungeon, trying to avoid detection, or we can approach the tower directly. Which do you prefer?"

1. If you want to go to the tower, turn to page 114.
2. If you want to sneak through the dungeon, turn to page 126.

"Gather about me closely," Pentegarn says. "Everyone hold on to my cloak. Jaimie, tuck Fox inside your shirt. Owl, hold on!"

Pentegarn closes his eyes and whispers some magic words.

You look down at your legs, and discover you no longer stand on the ledge. You are floating in mid-air!

"Great Zorn!" exclaims Baltek.

Pentegarn's eyes remain closed, and he continues to murmur words you do not understand. His staff points at the top of the tower, which is growing ever close. You close your eyes, not daring to look down.

After what seems like an eternity of flying, you gently bump onto the top of the tower. As soon as your feet touch the roof of the tower, Pentegarn collapses. All of the strength seems to have left his body.

You rush to his side, gasping, "Pentegarn, are you all right? Don't die!"

His eyes flicker open and rest on your face. "Would you care so much, Jaimie?" He pauses. "Don't worry, if I rest for a moment I'll be all right. But I'm glad you care, and perhaps this is the time to tell you something very important.

"Have you never wondered why you have abilities others do not—such as speaking with animals? Did you not feel a kinship the first time we met?"

You think back and realize all Pentegarn says is true. You nod your head.

Pentegarn continues, "The blood of kings and queens runs in your veins, for I am your great grandfather! I have little to offer you other than knowledge of your heritage, but if we live through this, I would have you become my apprentice. When we recover the staff, you will have much to learn, for one day it will be yours!"

Your eyes water, and you are near tears when Lydia suddenly screams, "Baltek! Where's Baltek?"

Leaping to your feet, you look about wildly. Baltek is gone! The only thing on the roof, other than yourselves, is a trap door, now lying open. You can see a ladder leading down the opening.

The elf rushes over to the ladder. "He's left us! He's gone off on his own! He'll take all the treasure!" She climbs over the edge of the hole and starts down the ladder.

"No! No, Lydia," you scream, tugging on her arm. "Come back! We have to discuss this."

"What is there to discuss? That accursed son of Zorn has gone off on his own, and he'll get everything before we do!"

"Lydia, calm down! He's our fighter. Maybe he's only gone ahead to check things out!"

"I'm the thief!" flashes Lydia. "If anyone checks things out, it should be me—not that big, clumsy, muscle-bound clod!"

"Lydia, even if he did find treasure, it's not likely he could—or would—just walk out the front door with it. He'll be back; we mustn't run off in different directions. Our only chance to win is to strike together."

"Tell that to muscle-brain!" mutters the elf, but she comes back up the ladder and sits with a flump at Pentegarn's feet.

"I still think we should go after him," snarls Lydia. "If he's not robbing us, he'll need our help."

1. If you think you should go after Baltek, turn to page 102.
2. If you think you should wait for Baltek to return, turn to page 72.

Fox's cries echo from rock to rock.

"That stupid animal will awaken every monster in the kingdom," Pentegarn mutters in great exasperation. "We'll have to rescue the blasted beast whether we want to or not. Curses!"

He turns and stomps off toward the shrieks.

As you start down the mountain, Owl says, "I've always warned Fox he doesn't deliberate long enough before he takes action. Haste makes waste, you know."

Fox's cries grow ever louder as you scramble down the broken piles of stone. Finally, you see two goblins poking at a dark hole with long pikes and a sword. The tip of Fox's tail lies on a rock outside the hole. You hear Fox yelping pitifully inside the hole. Each time he yelps, the goblins laugh loudly and thrust a sword or pike into the hole.

Without saying a word, Baltek and Lydia sneak up behind the goblins and dispatch them with two swift blows. Pentegarn drops down to his hands and knees, peering into the hole. "Stop your infernal screeching," he orders Fox. "Come out here now!"

A very dejected Fox creeps sadly out of the hole. Whimpering with pain, he crawls into your arms. He curls his squared-off tail under his belly and presses his muzzle under your arm.

"I hope you learned something, Fox!" Pentegarn says harshly. "We must stick together. Together we stand a fair chance, but alone we are doomed.

"Even more importantly, we must travel silently," he adds. "You were making enough noise to awaken the dead!"

As Pentegarn speaks, you hear a strange clacking coming up the slope. You have never heard such a noise before. It sounds like dead trees bumping against each other in a winter wind.

"Oh no!" whispers Lydia. "We have awakened the dead!"

An army of skeletons marches into view out of the darkness. Each carries a sword or polearm!

"A skeleton patrol!" whispers Pentegarn. "Some of those were my men, good and true, but now they answer the bidding of the Evil One. We must defeat them, or all is lost!"

"Jaimie, pick up a sword!" says Baltek.

You are not used to battle, but it appears you must fight or die. You take a sword from one of the fallen goblins.

The skeletons advance mechanically and soon reach you. Holding their swords stiffly in front of their bony bodies, they hack and slash continuously. You smash the first skeleton to pieces with one good blow as it comes into striking range. Even though

you destroy one skeleton after another, they continue to press forward, counting on their vast numbers to win the battle.

Finally, you and Baltek shatter the last two skeletons and the advance stops.

"That wasn't so bad!" you say.

"You think not, Jaimie?" asks Pentegarn, touching a skeleton with his foot. "Had they landed a killing blow, you would have become a skeleton in the Evil One's service."

You are overcome by shaking. How could you have forgotten?

"We shall have to be more than cautious," Pentegarn says. "For death at the hands of a skeleton means more than defeat, it means everlasting service to the Evil One."

With that, Pentegarn leads the way back up the mountain and onto the path. You are passing the ruins of an ancient building and nearing a large hole in the ground when you hear a loud outcry from behind you. Looking back, you see a patrol of goblins standing on a wall.

They pour down the wall and onto the path, screaming loudly.

You may:

1. Stay and fight; turn to page 10.
2. Run into the opening and try to lose them; turn to page 56.

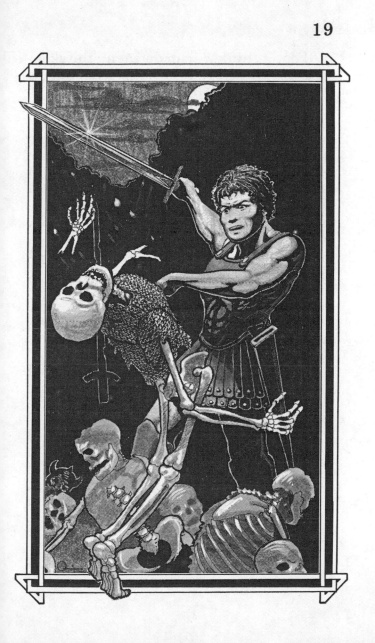

"I don't think we can defeat all the skeletons Baltek says are down there. Let's go up and try another way," you say.

Lydia quickly climbs the ladder into the room above. Pentegarn follows her slowly, but you and Baltek are right behind urging him on. As you start up the ladder, the first of the skeletons enters the room.

"Go ahead, kid!" Baltek says, "I'll hold them off."

Baltek jumps into the middle of the skeletons, swinging his sword mightily.

An evil laugh booms throughout the tower, and Lydia screams from above you. Pentegarn starts back down the ladder.

"Goblins, dozens of them!" screams Lydia.

Skeletons are pouring into the room below, and both Pentegarn and Lydia are trying to climb down the ladder. You are trapped!

Baltek is overcome by skeletons, but you can see he has taken over a dozen of the gruesome monsters with him. Looking up, you see goblins poking Lydia and Pentegarn with spears. Knowing you are doomed whether you stay on the ladder or not, you draw your sword and jump into the room of skeletons. You are determined to take at least as many of the foul monsters with you as Baltek did.

THE END

"With all due respect, sir," you say nervously, " do we have to go any of those ways? I'm not very good at fighting and bashing my way through things. And, to be honest, this sneaking business doesn't sound very pleasant either."

The thief flushes deep red and reaches for her dagger. Pentegarn puts out his hand and gently stops her action.

"Nor do I like the idea of going into a dungeon," you continue cautiously. "If something went wrong, we'd be trapped under the earth." A shiver of fear runs down your spine. "Isn't there some other way we could go?"

"Yes," Pentegarn says hesitantly, "I suppose there is. We could go over and through the ruins of my castle. It is a fairly direct route. Yes, yes, we could do that."

"If you please sir, that's what I'd like to do."

"A good choice, child. I should have thought of it myself. We'd best get started."

Holding the staff with both hands, Pentegarn taps the ceiling once, twice, three times. A section of it rumbles back to reveal the night sky.

"Away you go" says the fighter, boosting you through the opening. Soon, all of you stand outside the small hole. Pentegarn taps the ground gently and the missing sections fall neatly into place.

"Now," says the wizard, "we have two choices. We can go into the Hall of Kings, or we can go through a secret tunnel into the Hall of Past Glories. Which shall it be?"

1. If you choose the Hall of Kings, turn to page 36.
2. If you choose to go through the secret tunnel into the Hall of Past Glories, turn to page 32.

"l don't think we'd better try the magic stuff," Baltek says, "I wouldn't eat a cake that had been in the pantry for two hundred years. I don't think we'd be smart to mess with two hundred year old magic ingredients, either. We might get killed."

"All right Baltek, you've made your point," sighs Lydia. "Where do we go now?"

"Through that door," gestures the wizard. "It leads into the throne room. If the Evil One is here, that's where we'll find him."

"What are we standing here for?" asks Baltek. "Let's get on with it."

Baltek strides to the massive door and yanks on the handle. It does not open.

"Here, let me try," hisses Lydia. She works with the lock, but again nothing happens.

"It must be rusted shut," she snaps, stepping back and folding her arms.

Pentegarn steps up to the door and says, "Now stand aside, I have a door to unlock."

With a wave of his hand, the lock clicks and the door opens a crack.

Turn to page 84.

Choking back your fear, you duck under the pillars and enter the darkness. Glancing back, you see the goblins hard on your heels.

With the goblin cries echoing in the passage, you run as fast as you can, even though you have trouble seeing. Luckily, your long legs outdistance the goblins as you race down the corridor, but your breath soon rasps in your throat. You cannot last much longer without rest.

As you round the corner, a crumbling staircase rises upward into the darkness. The passage splits at the bottom and leads both left and right. You lean against the staircase and try to catch your breath, pressing your fingers against the stone wall. You feel ancient stone carvings under your hands. The cries of the goblins draw closer.

"Well, featherhead," pants Fox, "got any hot ideas now?"

"It is my astute opinion that—AWWWK!!"

The carving moves under your fingers and a section of the staircase opens without warning. You fall backward into darkness!

"Hey," Fox cries. "Wait for me!" He slips through the opening.

The wall quickly snicks shut and darkness closes around you. The dark is thicker and more complete than any you have ever known.

Goblin feet pound up the stairway you are hiding under, and then there is a long silence.

Finally, Fox says, "I don't know how to tell you this, but we're not alone."

"That is correct!" a deep voice says.

"Who's there?" you demand, trying to sound brave. In answer, a burst of light fills the room. A wrinkled old man leans on a staff in front of you.

He seems more ancient and frail than anyone you have ever seen. A bright, torch-like light leaps from his staff.

A young fighter stands on the old man's right, pointing his sword at you. His battle-scarred armor and bulging muscles tell you this is not someone to anger.

A beautiful elven maiden stands on the left. Bright red hair hangs to her waist. She wears carefully tailored leather armor. Her hand rests on a polished dagger handle, and she watches you intently with bright green eyes.

"Oh boy," mutters Fox. "We're in for it now."

"Patience, Fox," Owl says, "I have found hasty judgment leads to disaster."

"I can't think of anything more disastrous than dying," he answers.

"Fox! Owl!" cries the old man in a papery, dry voice. "Do not waste your strength arguing with each other. Neither the fighter Baltek nor the elven thief Lydia will harm you."

You stare in amazement as Fox and Owl stop arguing and walk across the floor toward the old man. They understood the old man and he understood them! "Surprised, child?" he asks. "Don't be. Like you, I can speak with animals, and so can those with me."

He pauses, and you back away from him.

"Do not worry, Jaimie," he continues, "I am not one to fear. Come. Sit beside me. I shall tell you and your friends everything you need to know."

He holds out his hand. His eyes are kindly and intelligent and hold all the strength his body lacks. Without a word, you cross the small space between you and clasp the waiting hand.

Fixing his gentle yet powerful gaze on you, he begins. "Although it seems unlikely, this was once a beautiful place. There were no goblins, no monsters, no death, no destruction. The fields were fertile. The people were prosperous and happy and blessed my name, the name of King Pentegarn.

"Although I was a wise and good king, I did not do it alone. I was aided by a great magical staff. It was given to me by my father, who had received it from his father before him, who had received it from his father before him. It contains the magic and knowledge of all of those lifetimes.

"Unfortunately, in the hands of evil it can be used with terrible results, as you see by this foul ruin.

"One night, as I slept, a black fog covered the kingdom. By the time we discovered this was a magical fog, it was too late. It had cloaked the coming of the Evil One. In the darkness of the magic fog, the Evil Master crept into my castle and stole my magic staff.

"When the sun rose, it could not pierce the black gloom. Most of my people fled in fear, and those who stayed to fight were killed by the black cloud. I fought desperately, but without my staff I was all but helpless.

"At last, I neared total exhaustion. All about me was ruin, and I was forced to leave my own kingdom. Though I was too weak to battle my unseen foe any longer, I vowed I would return.

"Year after year I have returned, seeking to defeat the Evil One and regain what is rightfully mine. This is my last attempt. The staff holds much of my strength and without it I grow ever weaker.

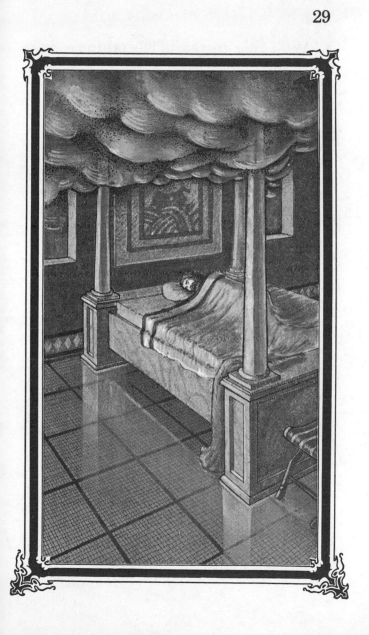

"Yet if I die, there will be nothing to stop the enemy." He pauses, then adds, "It must be stopped now, and you must help me!"

The old man stares intensely at each of you. As his eyes lock upon yours, you feel deeply drawn to him. His mission becomes yours. You believe, as the old man does, that you can, that you must, succeed.

Pentegarn continues, "The Master, as it calls itself, usually remains in the central tower. Between us and the tower are many halls, caverns, and passageways. They will be guarded by bands of goblins and skeletons, all of whom serve the Evil One.

"Although there are few ways to defeat the Evil One, I have a plan. A Cube of Mystic Forces and a Ring of Spell Turning lie hidden in the depths of the dungeon beneath the castle. I do not believe the Master possesses them. If we can get them, we stand an excellent chance of success."

"I don't agree with you," says the elf. "Wouldn't it be better to sneak straight through? We can avoid discovery as well as fighting, and perhaps pick up some treasure along the way."

"Me, I'm more in favor of a direct approach," says the fighter. "I suggest we move slowly, from one area to the next, fighting when necessary."

The old man fastens his gaze upon you.

"And you, little one?" he asks in a soft voice. "What do you think? Which of the ways would you choose?"

"M-m-me?" you stammer. "I'm just a kid. I don't know anything."

"Age has little to do with intelligence," replies the old man. "Do not take yourself so lightly. You and your friends have much to offer. What is your choice?"

1. You may choose the old man's course of action; turn to page 108.
2. You may choose the elf's way; turn to page 40.
3. You may choose the fighter's way; turn to page 7.
4. Or you may choose your own way; turn to page 21.

"Let's go through the tunnel," says Lydia, "I feel better underground. There are too many eyes above ground."

"Sounds good to me," says Baltek. "I like narrow areas myself; they're much easier to defend."

Fox agrees and follows behind the thief.

"Majority rules," says the elf firmly. "We take the tunnel."

"All right, then," says the wizard. "Follow me."

A cold wind whistles through the dark air as you pick your way over fallen columns, large blocks of stone, and shattered statues of ancient men. The black mouth of a tunnel looms ahead, and dread washes over you.

Hiding your fears, you follow the elf maiden into the darkness. Silence, thick and uncomfortable, swallows you. You feel as though evil, dark-loving creatures watch your every action. Your party bunches together around the dim light cast by Pentegarn's staff.

You have gone only a few yards when Owl says, "My superior eyesight tells me there is an obstruction directly ahead."

Not to be outdone, Fox adds, "My superior sense of smell tells me goblins are hiding behind that obstruction."

All eyes look to Pentegarn for direction. "There is no point in fighting them there," he says. "This path has been claimed by the Evil One. We will have to go on to the Hall of Kings, or return to the secret room under the stairs and choose another course of action."

1. If you choose to go to the Hall of Kings, turn to page 36.
2. If you want to return to the secret room and take another path, go to page 31 and choose any option except number 4.

"Let's stay here and smash them as they come out of the hole," you say.

"Good idea!" Baltek says. "Why didn't I think of that?"

As you speak, the first skeleton sticks its bony head out of the hole. Baltek quickly smashes it, and the skeleton falls back down. Like the mindless creatures they are, the skeletons continue to climb the ladder, and Baltek continues to smash them. A few manage to squeak past Baltek, but you and Lydia dispatch them quickly.

The skeletons keep coming, though you are certain you have slain at least fifty of the foul creatures. Finally, Baltek tires, and six of the creatures surge into the room. They attack Baltek immediately, and, though both you and Lydia swing your swords with all your might, you cannot save the mighty warrior.

When you have reduced the skeletons to nothing more than a pile of bones, Baltek lies dead beside the hole.

Lydia lets out a great moan, but Pentegarn quiets her.

"We must leave here before Baltek falls into the Evil One's service," he says. "We will grieve for him after we have taken our revenge."

Lydia refuses to move. "We're walking into a trap," she says. "The Evil One is down there with more goblins and skeletons waiting for us."

"I do not doubt you are correct," Pentegarn says. "But I do not see anything to do but meet the enemy."

"We should find another way into the chamber," Lydia says. "Perhaps a secret door."

"There were no secret doors when I owned this tower," Pentegarn says.

"That was a long time ago," snaps Lydia, "I wouldn't be surprised to find the Evil One has many secret doors where you had few."

"You may try if you wish, but I must meet the enemy now," Pentegarn says.

With that, Pentegarn climbs down the ladder.

1. If you choose to follow Pentegarn into the enemy's trap, turn to page 142.
2. But if you think it might be better to try to find another way into the chamber, turn to page 69.

"I choose the tunnel!" says Lydia.

You quickly cross to her side and say, "I really don't like being underground. Could we please choose the Hall of Kings? I know you'll understand, because even though you're as brave as Baltek, I'll bet there's something you don't like."

At first the thief glares at you, but her eyes finally warm. She smiles and says, "You're right. I can't stand bats. Just the thought of them makes my skin crawl. Let's go to your Hall of Kings."

You are soon threading your way between a line of jagged pillars. They rise high into the night sky.

"There used to be a roof connecting them," sighs the wizard. "It was really quite grand."

Thick swirls of sand muffle your footsteps as you march toward the ruins of a large chamber. A set of double doors, nearly twenty feet tall, hang loosely on their hinges.

"No need to knock," barks Fox. "Let's hope no one's home."

Slipping between the yawning doors, you find yourself standing in a wide corridor that stretches into total darkness.

"The hall of my ancestors," Pentegarn whispers. "How grieved they would be to see their kingdom now."

The rasp of steel on steel rings through the room suddenly. "Stand back," cries the fighter. "We are surrounded!"

You peer into the darkness, and you can barely see dozens of man-like shapes in the black room.

"No, dear fellow," Pentegarn says. "Put away your sword. There is no danger from this quarter. I will show you."

Pentegarn lights the room with his staff's flickering light, and you see statues stretching as far along the hall as you can see.

"Let me introduce my ancestors," says the old wizard proudly.

You approach the figures slowly and with a certain amount of dread. One by one, Pentegarn passes each figure and recites his or her name, telling of battles long past.

The first stone king holds a staff much like the one Pentegarn holds; a young and plain sapling with some carvings at its top. As you pass each king's statue, the staff grows and changes until it is a complex blend of beauty and power.

As you stand in front of the last statue, admiring the beauty and power of the staff, Pentegarn says quietly, "My father."

You notice, with astonishment, that Pentegarn's father wears an amulet that looks exactly like the one your mother gave you. You raise your hand to your chest, where the amulet still hangs under your shirt. Could it be the amulet Pentegarn's father wore?

As if reading your thoughts, Lydia asks Pentegarn, "What is that necklace?"

"That, my dear, is the Amulet of Power, a most wonderful device. Unfortunately, it was lost when the kingdom fell and I have not been able to recover it. If I had it, our job would be much easier."

As you are about to reveal the amulet to Pentegarn, a crazed howling fills the hall. You turn to see two large wolves running toward you. The beasts have glowing red eyes and ugly white teeth.

"Quickly," cries Owl. "There's not a moment to loose!"

Hearts racing wildly, all of you dash through the dusty darkness. The insane howling follows, lapping at your heels. You can see two doors ahead, one to the right and one to the left.

"Which way, old man?" Lydia shouts.

"A guardroom lies on the right and an antechamber to the left," Pentegarn gasps in answer.

Lydia quickly presses her ear to both doors. "I hear scurrying in the antechamber; nothing in the guardroom."

1. If you decide to enter the antechamber, turn to page 70.
2. If you decide to enter the guardroom, turn to page 88.

"I think we should follow Lydia's suggestion," you say.

"Good thinking, kid! I'll show you some fancy slinking. Follow me!" exclaims Fox.

"It does seem, indeed, this course of action may yield favorable results, although it is not without its own inherent perils," Owl says.

"You are a wise youngster," says the elf. Her dark green eyes beam approval.

The old man looks at you quietly. "So be it," he says in an old, soft voice. He gestures with his hands. Snick! The wall behind him opens into darkness.

"Come," he says. "The die is cast, and it is time for us to be upon our way."

All of you file past him and enter the darkness beyond.

As you leave, the wall slides shut behind you with a very final click!

You now stand outside, a brisk chill wind whistling about you.

"Watch it, kid," Fox yaps. "Your fingers are pretty nimble, but your feet aren't so hot!"

You look around and see you are walking a very narrow trail bordering the ruins of the kingdom. The remains of ancient buildings lie on your left, lit here and there by flickering fires. On your right you see a sheer fall. The edge of the mountain drops away only a few inches from the path!

Pentegarn stops and clutches your elbow. "There it is!" he whispers, raising a bony finger and pointing up the trail.

You see a tall black tower rising high against the night sky. As you study the tower, a terrible howl grows in the wind and hangs in the air. Shivers of terror run down your spine.

"That is our goal," the old man says. "Some of us may not survive our journey into it, but the mission is more important than our lives."

"Great!" says Fox. "Listen, kid, I just remembered I've got to rush home. See you!"

With that, Fox darts away down the trail.

Fox has not been gone more than three seconds before terrible screams tear the quiet of the night. "YIIII! YOWWWWL!"

"Fox! Fox!" you cry. Even louder screams answer your cries.

You have two choices. You may:

1. Rush down the trail into the dark and attempt to rescue your friend, no matter what danger faces you. Turn to page 15.
2. Consider the good of the entire party, rather than feelings for Fox. Turn to page 76.

"I say let's continue," you urge, "I don't want to go back."

You sneak through the doorway into the throne room.

At first you see nothing, then out of the darkness a bright red light appears. It soon turns clear white and arcs toward you.

As your eyes adjust to the light, you see a darkly robed figure sitting on a great throne. It clutches a great, glowing staff. You gasp with shock, for the same emblem you saw on the statue of Pentegarn's father is embedded on the head of the staff. It is the same emblem you bear on your amulet!

"Pentegarn," you say, "look!" You pull the emblem from under your shirt. But the old man has eyes only for his enemy. Pentegarn points his staff to do battle.

"Begone!" he booms. "Begone from my kingdom, and take your evil with you."

A flash of light shoots out of Pentegarn's small staff, but it dies when it reaches the Evil One.

Wicked laughter bursts from the figure. "I should have left my helpers behind. I won't need them to defeat you."

The Evil One waves his hand, and a dim light glows throughout the room. Only now are you aware of various creaks, clacks, squeaks, and growls of the armed skeletons, huge wolves, and horde of bats that surround the Evil One.

"You have plagued me too long, old man," the Evil One hisses. It points its staff and a thin beam of red light shoots at Pentegarn. The beam hits Pentegarn's staff and travels its length, shattering and burning the wood. After traveling through the staff, the beam strikes Pentegarn. The old man crumples to his knees, dropping his smoldering staff.

"Die!" screams the evil figure.

Pentegarn falls to the ground.

"No!" you cry. You run up the stairs toward the black figure, holding the amulet before you. A yellow beam shoots out of the amulet and locks onto the red beam coming from the Evil Master's staff. The red beam drops from Pentegarn's body immediately, and the great staff glows lemon yellow.

A shriek of pain erupts from the Black Master and a yellow glow bathes its body. It falls to the ground and starts growing smaller and smaller and smaller.

At last, whining and writhing, the thing on the steps disappears completely. At the same moment, the skeletons fall to the ground and shatter, no longer animated by their master's powers.

The rest of the room erupts with the sounds of battle. The wolves and bats battle Baltek and Lydia, who became visible with their first attack.

Suddenly, you realize you hold the Staff of Kings. It glows with a pale amber light that fills the large chamber. You point the staff in the direction of the fight, and a great light blinds you. When you can see again, the wolves and bats have fled, and Baltek, Lydia, and Pentegarn kneel at your feet.

"Please sir, don't do that," you say. "Take your staff back."

Pentegarn rises to his feet. Tears run down his cheeks, but he smiles with joy.

"It's not my staff, dear child. It is yours. The blood of kings and queens flows in your veins. If I had any doubts, they were dispelled by the amulet. No one can wear the amulet unless they are of our blood. You, Jaimie, are my great grandchild.

"You will raise the city to its former glory. Fear will be cleansed from the land, and you will rule wisely and well."

"Didn't you forget the part about riches and wealth beyond measure?" asks Lydia, sheathing her sword.

"You shall have them," you say, "if they are mine to give."

"Indeed they are, Jaimie," Pentegarn says, "indeed they are. Perhaps Baltek will even volunteer to lead your palace guard!"

"If you will have me," Baltek says, bowing, "I would consider it a privilege."

THE END

You back away from the dragon-skeleton, hoping Pentegarn can escape on his own. But, unfortunately, the skeleton opens its toothy mouth and lowers its huge head. Pentegarn tries to protect himself, but he falls to the ground as he backs away.

The monster grabs Pentegarn in its mouth. Realizing that Pentegarn is finished if you do nothing, you charge the monster, swinging your sword wildly. The skeleton lowers one great claw and grasps you. Your arms are completely trapped, and you cannot even move your toes.

Carrying you in its claw and Pentegarn in its mouth, the great dragon turns and moves back into the dark cavern. Looking back at your only hope, Lydia and Baltek, you see the creature's huge tail swish and send them flying across the room.

It looks like this is...

THE END

"I think we should try for the Cube of Mystic Forces," you say. "We'll need all the help we can get."

Without further comment, Pentegarn strides off down a corridor, and you all follow. Surprisingly, you meet no enemies. Soon, you stand in the cavern with the pillar that covers the cube.

Impatient, Pentegarn strides over to the pillar and grabs its base.

"What are you waiting for? Help me, Baltek."

Baltek quickly scrambles to Pentegarn's side. The two men grunt and groan. Sweat pours from both their brows, and finally the pillar rises. Lydia quickly snakes her hand underneath the pillar.

"I've got it!" she says.

She pulls the cube from beneath the pillar. Without even looking at it, she lays it aside.

As soon as she lays the cube on the ground, several goblins appear in the corridor at the edge of the cavern. They do not even hesitate; they charge straight at you and your friends.

Not pausing to think, you draw your sword and leap in front of your friends, none of whom are prepared to fight.

The charging goblins stop, frightened, as you brace yourself to fight. But their eyes quickly narrow, and they start to rush you.

"Leave little one!" a large goblin screams from the back, "Get cube! Master want cube."

The goblins rush. Not knowing what else to do, you throw your body at the front row of goblins. As your body thuds into them, they fall to the ground.

Before you can say "snazzlefrass," ten more goblins jump on the pile, not wanting to miss the fun of pinching and poking you.

"Get off Morg," one says. "You hurt."

The goblins curse and shout at each other, but the pile on top of you doesn't get any lighter. Many goblin hands pinch and squeeze you.

"Juicy," one says. "This one good to eat."

You try to struggle, but there are too many bodies on top of you.

The goblins suddenly quit pinching.

"Run away!" they scream, and bodies begin to pile off you. "Run away! Help, help! Light hurt."

Within seconds, you lie on the ground alone. You shield your eyes, for the room is filled with painfully bright light. Finally, you peek from under your elbow. The light is becoming fainter.

"Stand up, Jaimie," Pentegarn says.

You stand up and look at Pentegarn, or the man who should be Pentegarn. But instead of the stately gentleman who walked into the room, you see a man as tall as Baltek.

"Pentegarn?" you ask.

"Yes," he laughs, "I am restored to my full strength, thanks to your brave deed. Had you not thrown yourself at the goblin horde, they would have stolen the cube and all would have been lost."

You look about and see your friends are kneeling, their heads bowed. You do the same. Even Fox lays his head on his paws and is silent.

"Arise, my friends. We must move quickly. There is still much to be done."

Turning, Pentegarn races off down the corridor, and you follow in his footsteps.

Please turn to page 58.

"Gosh, I don't know," you say. "It's your kingdom and your magic stuff. If you think we should go for the cube first, how can I argue with you?"

"That's it kid," Fox yaps. "Stick with the power."

"This seems a most wise decision," Owl adds.

"Let us begin," says Pentegarn. He walks down a tunnel on the right.

"This was a wise choice, Jaimie," says Pentegarn. "I must admit I was worried you would make the wrong decision."

"What does my decision count?" you ask. "I'm just a kid who happened to come along."

"Nothing just happens, Jaimie. Nothing is ever really an accident. There is a grand destiny to our world, and your arrival was no chance happening."

You stare in wonder at the old man beside you.

"What do you mean?" you ask in a trembling voice. "Did you know I was coming?"

"Not really," answers Pentegarn. "Or rather, I did not know you were coming at this precise moment. But I did know it would happen. It was destined to happen."

You walk through a long, narrow tunnel lit by streaks of color.

"Pretty, isn't it?" asks Pentegarn. "You mix six liters of Oil of Rainbows with one liter of Ointment of Fireflies."

Soon, you walk into a cavern so high you can barely see the ceiling.

"Baltek," Pentegarn says, "I think we may need your services. The cornerstone lies in this cavern."

The walls of the huge cavern twinkle and glitter with brilliant streaks of color. In the center of the room an enormous, shiny block of stone sits. An equally large, shiny pillar rests atop the block. It rises high into the cavern.

"This is the Cornerstone of the Kingdom," says Pentegarn. "The Cube of Mystic Forces lies beneath it. We must not fail in our attempts to retrieve the cube, for once the pillar is moved, the Evil One will know we are here."

The fighter flexes his biceps and moves toward the cornerstone. He bends down and grasps the immense block. But before he can attempt to move the pillar, you hear a strange noise, as if someone were shaking a bunch of sticks together in a bag.

"Kid, I don't like the sound of this," says Fox. "How about checking out now?"

"Hush, Fox," you say. You strain to see what makes the strange noise.

The biggest skeleton you have ever seen stalks out of the gloom at the far edge of the vast cavern. It's a dragon skeleton! It must measure forty feet from the end of its toothy mouth to its last tiny tailbone!

It clacks toward you slowly.

Clutching your small sword, you leap in front of Pentegarn. Your knees are shaking, but the old man must be protected from the giant monster.

The fearful skeleton stops and stares at you. It has no eyes, but you feel the force of its sightless gaze as the head lowers.

Its sharp teeth glint in the rainbow light. Your knees shake harder.

Should you fight such a ferocious monster? It's awfully large, and the chance that you can defeat it is very small indeed. If you fight, you will probably be devoured by the skeleton.

But you are the only thing that stands between the monster and Pentegarn. If you flee, it will certainly devour Pentegarn.

1. If you decide the monster is too terrible, and that you stand no chance of defeating it, turn to page 46.
2. If you decide you must stand and defend Pentegarn at any cost, even if it means battling such a terrifying monster, turn to page 128.

"I think we should follow Lydia's suggestion," you say.

"So be it," says Pentegarn. "Follow me."

He leads you into a dark corridor with no exit. He raises his hands high above his head, points his fingers at the wall, and mutters some magic words.

Snick! The wall in front of him opens into the night. You walk outside and stand on a ledge high on the mountain. Ahead of you, a tall black tower rises high against the night sky.

"That tower is our goal," Pentegarn says. "Some of us may not survive our journey into it, but our mission is more important than our lives."

"Great!" says Fox. "I just remembered I have an appointment with the game warden."

With that, Fox darts away down the ledge. It happens so quickly you do not have time to stop him.

The night is torn by terrible screams almost immediately. "YIIIII! YOWWWWL! YIIII!!"

You have two choices. You may:

1. Rush down the rubble into the dark and attempt to rescue your friend, no matter what the danger; turn to page 15.
2. Consider the good of the entire party and follow Pentegarn up the ledge; turn to page 86.

"With that black fog, I don't think we stand a chance," you say. "I think we had better try to lure them in here."

"My thoughts exactly," Lydia says. "Here's my plan."

You listen to her plan, and put it into action quickly. Lydia jumps out of the hole leading into the tiny tunnel and screams, "What's the matter, tiny tots? Afraid to fight?" She climbs back into the small tunnel immediately.

Just as you had hoped, several goblins follow her. You and Baltek quickly dispatch them. After a short time, several more goblins enter the hole, and they, too, meet their doom.

But no more come. Finally, a goblin calls, "Morg, come out. Don't play games with Grog."

When no answer comes, Grog calls, "Grog's patrol go now. Leave heavy man for you to carry. Take his stuff to master. You learn to play games with Grog."

Hearing these words, you and Baltek wait for the goblins to leave and step into the large room. Pentegarn lies on the ground, bound and gagged.

You quickly free Pentegarn. His cloak is in tatters, and he has been stripped of everything of value he carried.

"Did they get everything?" you ask.

Pentegarn nods his head. "Everything except my staff. They left that over there," he points toward the far side of the cavern. "They thought it was a worthless stick." He looks broken-hearted, and once again his face has assumed the look of an old man.

"We shall have to try another way. The Evil One now expects us by this entrance. Give me my staff, please," he says, rising.

You fetch the staff and give it to Pentegarn. As soon as you hand it to him, his face loses some of its age, and he appears to grow a little stronger.

"Is this staff magical, too?" you ask.

Pentegarn nods. "Yes, but it is not as powerful as the Staff of Kings. Building a magic staff takes years, Jaimie, and requires the wisdom and learning of many wise men. This staff," he says, holding the small sapling out for you to see, "is much like you. It is just beginning its life, and it has much to learn. It can accomplish simple tasks, but we must take care not to demand too much of it. Now come, it is time for us to continue."

He walks back to the stairs, with you and the rest of your party following. After a long climb, you stand outside looking at a black tower in the distance.

"That is our destination," Pentegarn says.

Please turn to page 12.

"Quick!" says Pentegarn. "Run for that hole!"

You run as fast as you can, Pentegarn lagging behind.

You reach the hole ahead of the goblins, but as you plunge through, a black fog rises in the large cavern behind you. Lydia tumbles through next.

She screams, "Bats! I hate bats!" You help her beat a dozen ugly bats away.

Finally, Baltek jumps through the hole.

"Pentegarn?" you ask.

Baltek shakes his head.

"We'll have to rescue him," you say quickly.

"I'm for it, let's go get him!" Baltek urges.

"Not so fast," Lydia says, "I think we'd better use our brains, not our brawn."

1. If you want to do as Lydia suggests, turn to page 54.
2. If you don't believe you have time to set up the trap, and want to go after Pentegarn immediately, turn to page 107.

As you enter the doorway, you hear Fox screaming behind you. "Hey, wait for me! I'm coming too." He jumps in behind you, panting. You are astonished, but happy to see him.

Fox clears his throat with embarrassment, and, avoiding your eyes, says, "Hi guys! Bet you thought I ran away because I was scared, but I was really saving your bacon. My keen sense of smell picked up the scent of goblins, and I tricked them into chasing me instead of you, then lost them in the brambles. Please don't thank me... just remember how lucky you are to have me along."

Pentegarn looks at Fox slyly, but says, "Yes, we are certainly lucky to have you along. Come along, now. We have very little time."

Turn to page 137.

You follow Pentegarn through the confusing tunnels. After twenty minutes of endless wandering, Pentegarn stops. You are in a dark corridor ending in a bare dirt wall. There is a wooden trap door a few feet above your head.

"Where are we?" you whisper.

"At the foot of the tower," Pentegarn replies. "It is time to face our destiny."

No sooner has he uttered the words than the trap door flies open. All is dark beyond. Pentegarn grasps the edge of the doorway and pulls himself into the darkness with one swift movement.

You cannot let Pentegarn go alone. But, even though you leap, you cannot reach the opening.

"Here, Jaimie. Your heart is larger than you are," says Baltek.

Placing two large hands about your waist, he lifts you into the gloom above. Then he boosts Lydia and Fox up, following right behind them.

You are surrounded by silence, and you cannot see anything. "Maybe no one's here," you say hopefully.

"No!" hisses a deep, whispering voice. A brilliant, silvery light floods the room. The light springs from a staff of great age.

"Who's there?" cries Pentegarn. "Who dares hold the Staff of Kings—the staff of Pentegarn?"

59

A low laugh fills the room. "Don't you know me, Pentegarn? We've met often enough."

The light dims until it only glows softly. You now see dozens of skeletons and goblins, all armed and grinning, crowded against the far wall. The staff stands in the center of the room, glowing softly. A thick black cloud billows about its base.

As you watch, the cloud pulses and throbs as though alive. Then it mushrooms to enormous size, filling the room. Before your astonished eyes, the cloud turns into a large number of shrilling, chittering bats! They soar and wheel about your heads, the hot stink of their bodies filling your breath. You strike wildly at the furry creatures, but they deftly avoid your blows.

Lydia screechs in fear, swinging her fists madly at the bats circling her head. Finally, after what seems like an eternity of terror, the bats disappear and the swirling black fog replaces them. Gasping for breath, Lydia falls into Baltek's arms and clutches him tightly.

The black fog slithers and twists, growing larger and smaller. It snakes close enough to touch, then draws away. It spins like a small cyclone beside the staff and disappears. In its place stands a huge black wolf with fire-red eyes and long white fangs. The wolf whines and snarls, its belly close to the ground. Its back legs bunch beneath it, and it springs at you!

You throw your arms up to protect yourself from its attack, but the wolf disappears in mid-leap and the black fog returns.

Once more it twists and swirls, changing its size and shape with every breath. It moves back to its original spot beside the staff. Slowly, the form of a bent black figure clad in a black draping cloak emerges. The cloak covers it from head to toe. Its face is completely hidden. All you can see is a bit of swirling black fog—more terrifying than any face could be. It keeps its hands tucked inside the folds of its sleeves.

"As you can see," a hollow voice hisses from the depths of the hood, "I have many faces. I am darkness. I am fear. I am your worst nightmares." It pauses, the fog inside its hood rolling slowly, then continues in a thundering voice, "I command you to bow to my power! Your quest is hopeless!"

"No," shouts Pentegarn. "Not so long as I live!" He raises his young staff, a mere twig

Please, turn to next page.

compared to the Staff of Kings, and points it at the black figure.

A bright shaft of lightning blasts out of the end of the staff toward the enemy. But the figure raises its hand and points its staff at Pentegarn. Pentegarn's bolt stops in mid-air, trembles, and then retraces its passage. As the bolt strikes, it travels the length of the staff and explodes. Pentegarn's staff bursts apart and falls to the ground, shattered into a million smoking pieces.

"Do not try your petty tricks on me," the voice sneers. "How dare you challenge me when I have this?" It raises the mighty staff.

"I dare because I am the rightful king," Pentegarn shouts back. "And because I have this—and this!" So saying, Pentegarn opens his hand to reveal the pulsating Cube of Mystic Forces. At the same time, he raises his other hand and shows the ring. The tiny serpents twist and glide around his finger, hissing fiercely.

The Evil One hesitates, its smoky hands writhing around the staff slowly and thoughtfully. Finally, it speaks, "It has amused me to watch you live your life in hopelessness, but now you dare challenge me! None may live who do not bow to my power!" It points the staff at Pentegarn. "You no longer amuse me. Die!"

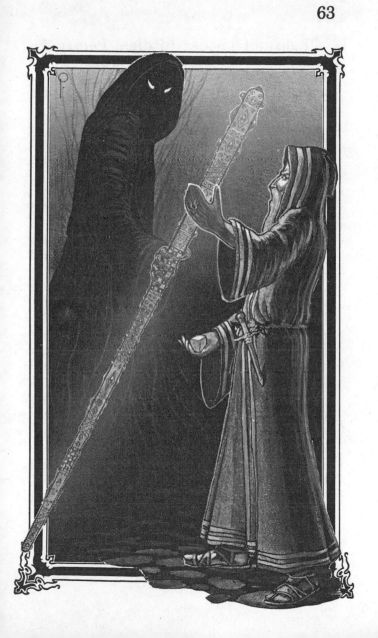

"I do not choose to die," Pentegarn answers calmly. He steps forward and grabs the Staff of Kings.

"Back! Back!" cries the dark figure. "Do not try!"

The staff glows dazzling silver, then dims to eerie red. It flashes silver once again, and begins to throb. The foes—one slight and frail, the other large and black—sway to and fro in the flashing light.

Suddenly, a tremendous boom echoes off the walls, and thick gray smoke fills the room. You begin coughing so hard you can barely stand. Even the goblins choke and wheeze.

When the smoke clears, you rub your burning eyes and strain to see the victor. You see the shattered remains of the skeletons, the bewildered goblins trying to find their master, and finally you see Pentegarn standing before you! The only sign the Evil One ever existed is a scorch on the floor.

Pentegarn turns his ring and staff toward the goblins and says, "I, Pentegarn, son of kings and rightful heir to this kingdom, command you to leave. I give you until morn to clear yourself and all your kind from my kingdom. Take nothing with you, and harm no one as you leave. Upon pain of unending death, I command this!"

The goblins trip and fall over each other in their haste to escape, literally dropping through the trap door.

Pentegarn turns his attention to you and your companions. But this is a new Pentegarn, so unlike the kind old man you grew to love. You find it difficult to meet his bold gaze. You quickly kneel, and your companions do the same.

"Come, Jaimie. Do not be afraid. I am still myself and so are you. We are still friends. Thanks to your loyalty and bravery, we have won. Now is a time for great rejoicing, great efforts, and new beginnings.

"Soon we will have a feast of celebration, and at that feast, we will celebrate more than the rebirth of a kingdom. We will celebrate the discovery of the heir to the staff and my kingdom!"

You look about in wonder.

"I suppose you mean me," says Fox.

Pentegarn's deep laughter fills the small room. "No, Fox. Modest and brilliant though you are, I am not speaking of you. I am speaking of one who is honest and true, loyal and brave..."

"Sure sounds like me!" mutters Fox.

"Whose veins carry the blood of kings and queens."

There is silence as everyone looks about in wonder.

"I am speaking of you, Jaimie. You are my great grandchild, the heir to the kingdom."

"Me? I'm your great grandchild?" you ask. "I'm your apprentice and your heir? Are you sure?"

"Yes, child, I am very sure. If you will continue to place your trust in me, I will take you as my apprentice and teach you all I know. One day the staff, the ring, and the cube will all be yours, as will the kingdom. So you must learn to be wise and strong now."

"If you've got so much to share," says Lydia, her hands on her hips, "how about us?"

"Yes," barks Fox, "I want my share."

"Can we afford a Fox muzzle?" asks Owl.

Pentegarn laughs, a great booming laugh, and says, "Lydia, Baltek, Fox, Owl, Jaimie; you will all share, and treasure is the least I have to offer. Come, my friends, gather round! We have much to discuss."

THE END

You fling yourself at the staff, praying you can knock it down and give your friends time to fight. You swing your sword ahead of your charge, hoping it will stop the goblins and skeletons before they reach you.

Before you reach the staff, however, three goblins throw themselves on you. One falls on your sword, but the other two grab your legs.

Pentegarn uses the confusion caused by your action to surprise the Evil One and grab the staff. The two struggle over the staff mightily, pushing and shoving each other into walls, causing the entire tower to shake.

Lydia springs into action, easily slaying one of the goblins who holds your legs. You slay the other. The two of you press your backs together and start swinging your swords at the horde of monsters.

Please turn to page 95.

As soon as his head disappears, the trap door slams shut.

You run to the door and start pulling on its handle, but it will not open. Lydia quickly searches the room for secret doors, but returns to your side almost immediately.

"I'm afraid he was right," she says. "There are no secret doors in this tower."

You both pull on the door with all your strength. It pops open, sending you flying.

In the room below, you see Pentegarn struggling with a bent black figure. Pentegarn holds one end of a mighty staff, and the black figure's smoky hands hold the other end. They are surrounded by dozens of goblins and skeletons.

With your sword swinging, you jump into the middle of the horde of monsters. Lydia quickly follows.

Please turn to page 95.

Baltek charges to the door of the antechamber and opens it. "If we spend any more time discussing the problem, we'll soon be dead. Let's have more action and less debate!"

"That's my kind of talk!" says Fox.

"Of course, one would expect you to approve of that sort of foolish sentiment," Owl comments.

"Quit hooting, Owl, or I'll tie your beak in a knot!" growls the fighter. "Hurry, help me barricade the door we came in!"

Aided by the glow of the wizard's staff, all of you pile rocks and beams against the door.

Two heavy thuds crash against the door, and the air is filled with howls and growls. The door shakes continuously under the attack of clawed feet. But it holds and at last the monsters withdraw, whining in frustration.

Baltek lowers his sword and heaves a deep breath. "Now we can go on. I wouldn't want them on our trail for long!"

"We are in the entrance to the Grand Council Chambers," Pentegarn says. "The door in front of us leads to the council chambers, and the door to our right leads to the guard rooms."

"I still hear squeaking and rustling in the council chambers," says Owl.

1. If you enter the council chambers, turn to page 82.
2. If you enter the guard room, turn to page 88.

You sit in silence for a long time.

Finally, you hear noises at the foot of the ladder. Lydia draws her dagger and you pull out your sword. Pentegarn stumbles to his feet and leans heavily upon his staff. You hear heavy breathing, then a head and shoulders appear.

Lydia screeches, "It's Baltek! That pig-dog, he better not have any treasure!"

Baltek pulls himself onto the tower roof. Blood oozes from a small cut on his forehead.

"Sorry to keep you waiting," he says.

"Did you find any gold?" demands Lydia.

"I only made it to the second room," he answers, "I climbed into a goblin ambush." He draws his sword and runs his finger along its edge. "But I finished them off before you could say Baltek-the-Great!"

"Did you get all of them?" Fox asks.

"Well," Baltek hesitates, "one did sneak away, but he was bashed up pretty good."

"Great," Lydia snaps, "now the Evil One knows we're coming."

"He knew we were coming, anyway," Pentegarn says. "Now he knows to fear us. Let us give him more to fear!"

With that, he leads the way down the ladder into the tower. You cross one empty room, and climb down another ladder into a room full of dead goblins. The scene is impressive, indeed. At least twenty dead goblins lie scattered throughout the chamber.

As you study the scene, the most terrifying laugh you have ever heard rolls through the opening leading into the other room. Baltek starts down the ladder first, but as soon as his head disappears, you hear a mighty scream of fear. Baltek's head reappears immediately, followed by the rest of his body.

"There are more skeletons down there than in any graveyard!" he says.

"Let's get out of here!" Lydia screeches.

"But we're so close," Pentegarn sighs. "It seems a pity to leave now."

"It's better to leave and try another route than to wait for those fellows to get us," Baltek says.

1. If you want to run back up the ladder and try to get off the tower before the skeletons catch you, turn to page 20.
2. But if you think you can make your stand here and defeat the skeletons, turn to page 34.

You quickly turn and run back up the steps. "Let's get out of here," you call. "We'll find another way."

Your friends follow, but Baltek soon stops and grabs a great boulder. "Go on!" he calls, "I'm going to slow them down a little."

You run up the steps, and Baltek follows two seconds behind, carrying the boulder. Twenty feet up, Baltek stops and turns around. You turn around, too.

He rolls the boulder down the stairs. The goblins stop in their tracks, frozen with fear. Those in the front rows scream "Run away! Run away!"

The goblins in the back rows, protected by the bodies of their companions in front, press forward. "Coward!" they scream, ignoring the cries of the goblins caught in the boulder's path. "Come back! Fight!"

Despite the fact that the boulder killed many goblins, you have no desire to fight those who remain. They chase you up the stairway, though they are slowed considerably by the boulder and the other goblins lying in their path.

You run to the top of the stairs and out into the night. Ahead, you see a tower glinting in the moonlight.

Please turn to page 12.

You decide the good of the party must come before the good of an individual. But Fox begins to shriek and whine even more loudly, and you turn to rush to your friend. The heavy hand of the fighter grasps you firmly by the shoulder.

"You cannot go, Jaimie. Fox was unwise, but he made his own decision. No one forced him to leave," Pentegarn says. "You cannot endanger the party by attempting his rescue. We must leave him to his fate."

Still struggling, you are hurried off down the trail. Fox's cries fade away, but they have been engraved upon your heart in pain.

You continue down the narrow wall until it meets the mountain. Soon, you must edge along the trail, spreading your arms flat against the mountain to balance your movement. Progress becomes very difficult to make.

At long last, the ledge ends in a wide rock shelf. "The worst is over," Pentegarn says. "We are about to enter the great cavern, and our path will be much easier."

He turns and faces the blank mountain wall, which rises smooth and unbroken. Raising his arms, he begins to chant.

A doorway grinds open where seconds before there was only solid, unbroken rock. You can see two passages going into the mountain.

"Come, friends, we have no time to lose. Fortunately this will be an easy route."

You are eagerly heading for the doorway when a long low growl stops you short. Four huge dog-like forms slink toward you from inside the mountain. But these are not dogs; they're wolves! Foam drips off their long, white fangs. Their faces are hideous, snarling masks of evil. Their eyes glow like embers in a firepit.

"If this is going to be easy," hoots Owl, "I'd hate to see it get hard!"

The wolves slink closer, and one leaps at you with a deep, threatening growl.

You have nowhere to go. The sheer edge of the mountain lies behind you, and the trail is too narrow to flee upon!

You are slowly backing toward the doorway when a wolf jumps on your back, knocking you to the ground. You roll over and look into the mouth of a vicious wolf. Its glowing red eyes drill into yours, and its hot breath beats upon your face. It leans forward for a deadly bite.

Then you hear a great flapping of wings. It's Owl! He is trying to draw the wolf's attention from you by attacking the evil creature. You roll away and press yourself against the doorway. Owl locks his talons into the wolf's head, and the ugly creature snaps and snarls with pain and rage. It whips its head from side to side, trying to shake the determined bird.

Just as you fear the wolf will free itself from Owl, Baltek rushes up and kills the enraged creature with one blow from his mighty sword. Owl falls to the ground and lies battered but breathing on the ledge. The fighter, too, bleeds from many wounds.

"Thank you, Baltek!" you say, "Owl and I both owe you our lives."

The fighter nods, but has no energy left to reply. You look about the ledge. All of the huge beasts have been slain, but at great expense. Lydia lies beneath a wolf, her dagger buried in the great beast's heart.

Pentegarn is collapsed against the wall. A wolf lies dead at his feet, burned to a crisp. Fearing the old man is dead, you slowly approach his crumpled form.

All is not lost — he lives! As you lean over him, the old man whispers, "What injuries have we taken?"

"I'm all right, and so is Owl, but Baltek bleeds badly, and Lydia may be dead."

"Well, we must see what we can do," he says tiredly. "Please hand me my staff."

You pick up his staff and give it to him, then drag the body of the huge wolf off Lydia. She is covered with blood and lies very still on the cold ground.

Leaning down, Pentegarn cries, "Quick! There is life; we are in time. Hold her up, Jaimie!"

Pentegarn draws forth a vial of smoky fluid. It shifts within the clear glass as though it has a life of its own. He carefully pours the precious potion between the thief's lips, a drop at a time. For one breathless moment, nothing happens. Then, at last, Lydia opens her eyes. She has the look of faraway visions in them.

"Pentegarn," she sighs, "I'm so glad you're not a wolf!"

"So am I," chuckles the old man. "So am I! Now rest for a moment, my dear. You'll be all right soon. I must see to Baltek."

Though the fighter's wounds are bloody, they are less serious and Pentegarn quickly tends to him. At last everyone is cared for, and you notice that the edge of the doorway ripples and wriggles like a reflection on water.

"Quick!" cries Pentegarn. "The spell is losing its power!"

Helping Lydia and Baltek, you hurry through the opening. The boulders grind shut behind you. You were just in time!

1. If you choose the corridor on the right, turn to page 57.
2. If you choose the ledge on the left, turn to page 86.

"I'm not afraid of rustling and squeaking," says Baltek. "I say we go through this door." He opens the door. Instantly, Owl glides off your shoulder into the room.

You hear tiny terrified shrieks and wild scamperings. Then Owl glides out of the darkened room and lands at your feet. A dead mouse dangles from his beak.

"I believe this solves the question of rustlings," he says in a dignified tone. "Mus musculus, I believe. I don't think it will prove to be much trouble. If you'll excuse me, I'll dispose of it." Owl's head swirls around with a quick gulp.

"There's something else in the room, mouse-breath," says Fox. "Up there near the ceiling. I can hear it, but I can't see it."

Pentegarn lifts his staff and the bright white light falls upon a wriggling mass of black and brown bodies. High-pitched shrieks ring out as the creatures circle and wheel about the room.

"Bats! I hate bats!" screams the thief. "Why did I ever listen to you, Jaimie? We should have gone through the tunnel."

"Calm down my dear. I'll take care of them," says the wizard. He raises his staff once again and the creatures wheel toward the corners and away from the dazzling light. The wizard points his staff at the two largest masses of bats and two fireballs hurtle toward the ugly creatures, which then fall dead upon the ground. "You see," says Pentegarn, "there's nothing to worry about. You might say I have a way with animals."

"Good work, Pentegarn!" says Baltek.

"Let's get going," Fox snaps impatiently.

"Quite right, Fox," says the wizard. "The two doors you see before us lead to the guardroom and the alchemist's laboratory. There may be a small amount of magic left in the alchemist's chambers, but it's hard to say after all these years."

1. If you wish to enter the guardroom, turn to page 88.
2. If you wish to enter the alchemist's chamber, turn to page 98.

"Here, let me splash a little fluid of invisibility upon us," says Pentegarn. He fumbles through his robes, searching for the container.

"Are you sure it'll work?" Baltek asks anxiously.

"How long does it last?" Lydia asks nervously.

"It will work just fine," the magic user says reassuringly. "It will last long enough for us to accomplish our mission.

The wizard carefully pours several drops of the liquid on the tongues of Lydia and Baltek. They disappear into thin air!

"Not bad at all," Lydia says gaily. The voice is directly in front of you, but you see nothing. Suddenly, invisible fingers dig into your ribs and tickle you.

"Stop it, stop it! I hate being tickled," you scream. Trying to escape the persistent tickling, you roll across the dusty floor and bump into Pentegarn. You hear a tinkle and a poof. Gasping, you open your eyes and see Pentegarn wringing his hands. He looks down at the floor glumly.

"I had just sprinkled Fox and Owl when you bumped me," he frets, "I dropped the vial and it broke. Fox got a double dose and I'm afraid there's nothing left for us."

"Does that mean I'm this way forever?" yaps Fox.

"We could not possibly have such great fortune," Owl says.

"No, it's not permanent," says the wizard. "But this accident might alter our plans considerably. Maybe we should go back and choose another path."

1. You can go back to the secret room under the stairs and pursue another course of action; turn to page 31 and choose any option except number 4.
2. Or you can continue on this course of action and take your chances; turn to page 43.

You are nearing the end of the ledge when Pentegarn halts. Suddenly Baltek draws his sword and raises it for a mighty blow. Something creeps toward you.

"Stop! Stop!" you shout, "It's Fox!" A bedraggled Fox crawls out of the gloom.

"Hi!" he says, avoiding your eyes. "I smelled an army of skeletons coming up the trail, so I went back to take care of them. You should have seen me outwit those numbskulls! There were hundreds of them, marching up the trail one after the other, carrying battle-axes and spears. I led them on a wild-goose chase down the mountain, then circled back here! Aren't you lucky to have me along?"

Pentegarn studies Fox a moment, then laughs and says, "Yes, but I hope you do not plan to leave us on our own again. In fact, your return comes at the right time. We now face a major decision.

"The ledge ends here. To our left a stairway leads down into the dungeons beneath the castle ruins.

"To our right a stairway leads directly to the tower. That way is more direct, but it will be more dangerous. What shall we do?" You may:

1. Take the longer route through the dungeon; turn to page 126.
2. Or attempt to go straight to the tower, turn to page 114.

The door to the guard's chamber proves difficult to open. Muted grating noises echo through the room; the sounds of beams and rocks shifting. You all squeeze through the door quickly and it slams shut.

"Quick, everyone," shouts Lydia. "Get away from this door!"

Seconds later, a thick cloud of choking dust fills the room, and a loud roar shakes the floor. When the air clears, you see that the doorway is nearly buried under a mountain of dirt, rocks, and beams.

Taking a deep breath of relief, you examine the room by the glow of Pentegarn's staff. Shields, swords, daggers, and other instruments of war lie about the room.

"Here kid, take this sword," the fighter says, placing a weapon in your hand.

"I don't know how to use this," you say, trying to lift the heavy thing.

"Forget the sword, kid," says Lydia. "Use this, I had one when I was your age."

She places a small, beautiful dagger in your hand. You slide it into your belt. "I don't know how to use this either," you say. "But at least it's the right size. What do we do now?"

"We can open the door on the right and slip into the council chambers," Pentegarn says.

"Where Lydia heard the rustling and scurrying," Owl croaks.

"Or we can venture into the alchemist's room," Pentegarn says. "I seem to remember, too, that there was a door to the ante-chamber hidden on this side of the wall, but I can't remember where."

"Two choices are enough for me, wizard," says the fighter. "Any more than that confuses me."

1. If you wish to enter the council chambers, turn to page 82.
2. If you wish to enter the alchemist's lab, turn to page 98.

Pentegarn scurries about the room peering into bottles and jars. Finally, he says, "Baltek and Lydia, give me your weapons."

"What for?" Baltek asks cautiously.

Pentegarn pulls an old trunk over to the work bench and rummages through it, pulling out several yards of silk scarves, a stuffed rabbit, and a vial of pink liquid. Finally, he answers Baltek, "If all goes well, I shall make your blades unbreakable and as sharp as a razor for all eternity."

"Sounds good to me," says the fighter. "But do it quickly. I feel naked without my sword."

Pentegarn pours a blue liquid onto the blades, then murmurs some magic words. Blue smoke billows over the blades. "If my memory serves me right," Pentegarn says, "I should add a drop of Pink Oil of Permanence, and all will be done!"

He pours a drop on each blade, and there is a very loud poof! A streak of silvery pink shoots straight to the ceiling, staining the wizard's beard as it passes. "Oh my, I don't remember that," he says.

He stares through the pink clouds shrouding the table. "What did I do wrong?" he asks, puzzled. "I don't remember it smoking before."

You follow his gaze down to the blades. They are pitted, crumbling, and worst of all, pink.

"What have you done?" cry Baltek and Lydia angrily.

"That never happened before," Pentegarn says absently. "Isn't that amazing!"

"You'd better figure it out fast!" growls Baltek. "We're easy targets for the Evil One without our weapons."

"It's quite hopeless," Pentegarn mutters glumly. "I can't repair these blades." He begins rummaging through the chest at his feet again, "I'm afraid you'll just have to settle for new ones."

When he rises, he holds a set of new weapons.

"Feels all right to me," Baltek says, slashing through the leg of the workbench.

"Since that didn't work," Lydia asks, sheathing her blades, "where do we go from here?"

"The throne room lies just beyond the next door," answers the wizard. "It is possible he whom we seek lurks there."

"Why didn't you say so?" screeches Lydia. She tromps off toward the door.

"Wait!" you say, drawing the amulet from beneath your shirt, "I have to tell you something." But no one is listening. The wizard draws himself up as tall as he can, points at the door, and whispers a magic word. The door opens.

Turn to page 84.

The Evil One points its staff. "Kneel before me!" it thunders.

With a gasp of outrage, Pentegarn flings himself at the staff.

"Back, back!" cries the dark voice wildly. "Do not try!" It tries to evade Pentegarn's rush, but Pentegarn is too fast. He reaches out and grabs the glowing staff with both hands. The dark figure tries to pull the staff back with its smoky, wispy fingers.

The staff turns dazzling silver, then dims to an eerie red. It flashes silver once again, and seems to vibrate and throb. The two foes—one slight and frail, the other large and black—sway back and forth in the flashing light. A tremendous boom echoes off the walls, and dirty gray smoke fills the rooms. You cannot see anything and are coughing so hard you are barely able to stand. Even the goblins choke and wheeze.

When the smoke finally clears, you rub your burning eyes and strain to see the victor. There is no dark figure, but there is no Pentegarn either—and no staff. Nothing remains of their presence except a great scorched mark in the center of the room.

The skeletons are nothing but piles of bones along the walls, but a great wailing goes up from the goblins. "Master gone! Master gone!" You and Lydia look at each other. You are the only two left, except for Owl and Fox. Drawing your weapons, you slowly retreat until your backs are against the wall. The angry goblins begin their approach, weapons drawn.

A sudden rage fills you as you think of Pentegarn and Baltek. You leap forward, waving your sword and screaming a loud war cry. Lydia, after a startled glance, follows your lead and the battle is on.

You wield your sword with great skill and determination, vowing that no matter what, you will keep swinging until...

THE END

Four skeletons attack you and Lydia, their swords swinging in slow, deadly arcs. You dodge the blows, landing a hit of your own on one of the foul monsters. It clatters to the floor in a heap of useless bones.

Lydia quickly strikes a skeleton with her sword and kicks another. Both of those skeletons fall, and, quick as a cat, she delivers a nasty blow to the skeleton attacking you. It clatters to the ground, and the two of you turn to face the rest of the monsters, pressing your backs against the wall.

Four more skeletons take the place of the four you have slain. But now the goblins, too, are ready for battle. They approach you from the side, jabbing at you with their polearms.

"We are doomed!" Lydia cries, swinging her sword in a wide, mad arc.

Looking up from his own struggle, Pentegarn sees your trouble and gives the Evil One a mighty shove. The bent black figure falls backward in surprise, and Pentegarn swings the Staff of Kings high in the air, calling powerful magic words.

A clap of thunder roars through the room, and a blinding light assaults your eyes. You cannot see or hear anything for several seconds.

When you can see and hear again, the room is empty except for you and Lydia. There is a scorch mark where Pentegarn and the Evil One fought, and dozens of broken skeletons litter the floor. The goblins are nowhere to be seen.

"Did we win?" you ask.

"I'm not sure," Lydia says. "But the Evil One is gone."

"And so is Pentegarn," you add sadly. "What are we supposed to do now, rebuild the kingdom? I sure wish we had Pentegarn here to help."

"He gave everything he had to save us, Jaimie," Lydia says, "I guess that means he trusted us to do the job."

"Do you think we'll be good rulers?" you ask, starting to climb back out of the tower.

"What's this 'we' business?" snorts Lydia. "You be the ruler. I'm not cut out for that sort of stuff. Just give me a ton of your treasure, and I'll be happy."

"Well, I'll help you rule," Fox says, "I'll be your treasurer. I'm always good at spending other people's money."

THE END

"This was my favorite room," says Pentegarn. "Let's see if we can find a few useful trinkets lying around."

He looks about and picks up a fancy crystal bottle. "Excellent!" he says, shaking the bottle and peering into it. "I wonder if there's any left. It's so difficult to tell with invisible potions." The wizard places his finger over mouth of the bottle and tilts it. The finger disappears!

"Wonderful, wonderful!" cries the wizard. "I was so afraid it had evaporated."

"What happened?" you cry in alarm.

"Nothing to worry about child," Pentegarn reassures you. "This is Essence of Invisibility. It could come in quite handy, but I will have to be careful not to break the bottle. I don't want to disappear quite yet."

"If you found that," says Lydia, "I bet you could find other magic things, too."

"You're right Lydia. Maybe I could find something magical for you! But the materials in my workshop have been here for centuries, and many of the ingredients have become unstable. It would be dangerous to use them. So you must all decide what you wish to do."

1. If you wish to conjure forth another magical item, risking the possibility of a magical accident, turn to page 90.
2. If you want to continue on this course without trying to manufacture more magical items, turn to page 23.

"I'll do it," you say.

"I'll show you a shortcut to the Pillars," Fox volunteers.

"Allow me to ride on your shoulder, Jaimie," Owl says, "and I, too, shall accompany you."

You hold out your arm and Owl climbs up to your shoulder. Following Fox, you enter the forest.

After twenty minutes, you come to a tall stand of ash trees. Brambles and briars grow entwined around the base of the tall, gnarled trees. You push your way through, and see that the forest stops at your feet. The ground in front of you is a sickly burnt gray.

Several large pillars rise like thick white fingers from the blackened earth. Their tops are broken and jagged, and huge pieces lie strewn about the clearing.

An opening gapes near the base of the pillars like a missing tooth in a jack-o-lantern. You see three sets of foot prints leading into the opening.

As you peer into the opening, a squeal breaks from the forest, and you turn to see the goblins racing from the tangles.

Please turn to page 24.

Much as you would like to believe Baltek is merely scouting in advance, you secretly fear Lydia is correct.

"We must hurry if we intend to catch him," you say. "He doesn't stand a chance alone."

Pentegarn sighs, "I have not yet regained my full strength. But I shall do my best."

"Lydia," says Pentegarn. "You lead the way."

Lydia disappears down the ladder in a flash. Your heart pounding in your chest, you tuck Fox under your shirt and follow Lydia. You all gather at the foot of the ladder. Little light filters down the small opening, but there is enough light for Owl to see there is no one else in the room.

"There's another opening and ladder over there against the wall," croaks Owl.

As soon as you set foot upon the ladder, your skin prickles with the knowledge that somebody waits in the room below. You expect a blade in your back at any moment, but nothing happens and you soon stand on the floor.

"Over here!" Lydia whispers harshly.

"Let's see what we've got here!" says Pentegarn, and a dim glow from the tip of his staff fills the room. The sight is as awful as any you can imagine. Two dead goblins lie on the floor, their wounds showing the fighter passed this way. However, he could not have passed unharmed, for there is

Please turn to next page.

blood on their swords. A trail of blood leads to the next ladder.

"Quick," says Pentegarn. "We have no time to lose. Hurry!" His staff lit and leading the way, Pentegarn climbs down the ladder, all signs of weakness gone. Lydia follows, and you hear her let out a great wail almost immediately. Fearing the worst, you hurry down the ladder to find your fears have come true. Baltek lies propped against the wall, hideously wounded. Several goblin arrows stick out of his armor. The fighter is breathing his last.

"At least I took them with me," gasps Baltek.

For the first time, you notice that the floor is strewn with bones...lots of them.

"Skeleton patrol," gasps Baltek. "Don't worry, they didn't touch me. It was the goblins who did me in—them and my own stupidity.

"I was standing in the tower when I felt a pull of power such as I have never felt before. I realize now it was testing me, and I foolishly accepted the challenge. At first I set out to conquer it alone. As I progressed, a strange thought came over me. 'If this power is so great,' I thought, 'it is a greater power than ours, and we are doomed to failure.' I decided to offer my services to it. Then I, too, would enjoy great power and wealth. I would be unbeatable!

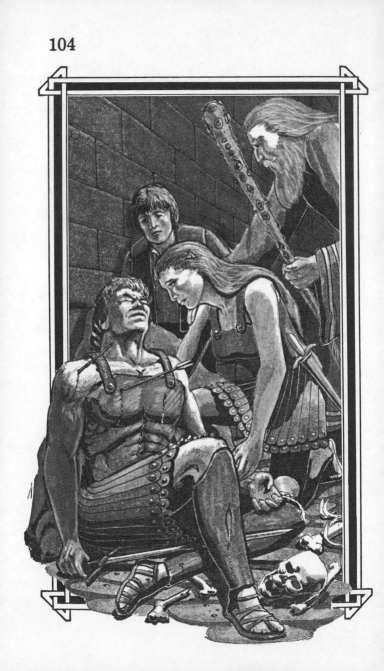

"At that moment, I heard a burst of laughter in my mind. The Evil One had bent my thoughts. It had no need of me or my services. As soon as I realized my mistake, my mind was my own once more. But then the goblins appeared, followed by the skeletons. I won, but at great cost, as you can see. I went as fast as my strength could take me. I had betrayed you, but at least I could destroy some of the enemy. All I can say is...I'm sorry."

Pentegarn says, "I fear the die was cast long before we reached this tower. It is I who must apologize. Yet, we may succeed because of your bravery. Be at peace, Baltek."

The light steals from his eyes and a great calmness comes over his features...Baltek is dead.

"A great man has died," Pentegarn says softly.

You have no time for further mourning. A howling fills the air, and a trap door at Baltek's side crashes open. A flurry of bats explode through the opening.

"I think the Evil One has extended his invitation," Pentegarn says.

"We're walking into a trap," Lydia snarls.

"You are quite right, my dear," Pentegarn says. "But I fail to see any other choice."

"Perhaps we can trap the trapmaster," Lydia says. "He expects us to come in full force. We can send Pentegarn down alone, then search for another way into the chamber and surprise the Evil One."

"That is a good plan," Pentegarn says. "But it has one fault. There was no other way into that chamber when I ruled this tower."

"Besides that, we don't even know if the Evil One is in the next chamber," you add quickly.

"You can bet your jerkin he's down there," Lydia says. "And if we can't find a secret door, we'll come down the ladder a few minutes later than Pentegarn. Anything is better than letting the Evil One trap all our forces at once."

"Do what you must," Pentegarn snaps, "I must meet my destiny!"

The wizard quickly climbs down the ladder.

It's your decision.

1. If you want to go down the ladder with Pentegarn, and hope your party's strength is enough to withstand the Evil One's trap, turn to page 142.
2. If you would rather try to spring a surprise of your own on the Evil One, turn to page 69.

"Let's quit wasting time," you say, climbing out of the hole into the black fog. Baltek quickly follows, swinging his mighty sword. Lydia joins you almost immediately, and Fox and Owl sneak out of the hole quickly.

Before you can say "Over here," hundreds of black bats swirl around your head. You quickly lose sight of Baltek and Lydia. You swing your sword madly, hoping to hit anything that is trying to hit you. You hope Lydia and Baltek are far enough away that you won't hit them.

Finally, several rough hands grab you. You turn, swinging your sword. You feel it connect and hear a body fall.

"He kill Snaffle!" a goblin says. Many more hands grab you, wrenching the sword from your grasp.

"I tell you they come back out, Morg."

"You smart goblin, Grog. Master reward you."

The goblins quickly tie you and lay you next to Baltek, Lydia, and Pentegarn. You hear Owl and Fox squawking in the bags two goblins carry.

A goblin pokes you, then several goblins pick you and your friends up. They walk toward their tower. It looks like...

THE END

All eyes rest on you. "Since this is your kingdom," you say, "and you have tried other methods before, we should go the way you suggest."

"Let's get on with it," says the fighter. "How do we get out of here?"

"Like this," says Pentegarn. He taps the floor with his staff and the stone disappears. A dark hole appears in the floor.

"This chute will take us into the dungeon, where the cornerstones of the castle lay. The cube lies hidden beneath one of them.

"The ring lies atop a pillar rising from the second cornerstone."

"Too much talking," grumbles Baltek. "Let's get started."

He draws his sword, dangles his feet over the edge of the hole, and disappears into the darkness.

"A man of action," says Pentegarn, as he lowers himself into the hole and is swallowed by the gloom.

"Last one in is a goblin!" cries Lydia. Holding her nose, she leaps in after Pentegarn.

"Let's go, kid," urges Fox. "Don't be a stick in the mud!"

You ease over to the hole and peer in, but see nothing. You dangle your feet into the blackness. Fox climbs onto your lap and Owl sits on your shoulder.

You take a deep breath, close your eyes, cross your fingers, and push off. It's like flying! You're moving so fast it feels like you're on a giant glass slide.

"This is fun!" says Fox. "Let's do it again!"

You land with a thump, dropping Fox and Owl onto the floor. You look up dazedly to find yourself kneeling between friend and foe. Lydia stands behind you with her dagger raised. Pentegarn holds his staff with both hands, and Baltek has drawn his sword. Four goblins and two wolves stand opposite your friends. A black cloud of bats swirls above them.

Scrambling backward, you join your party and watch the enemy approach.

Baltek throws you a short sword, crying, "Use this, Jaimie!" Then the mighty warrior races forward, hacking and slashing at the goblins. One falls immediately, but you don't have time to watch. A wolf leaps straight at you!

You step aside quickly, jabbing your sword at its furry hide as it passes. It turns and snarls, its red eyes flashing with rage. The creature creeps toward you. Deep growls rumble from its throat, and foam drips from its long white fangs. It springs at you again.

The great beast lands full upon you, and you fall backward. Its shaggy black fur covers your face, and its weight pins you to the ground. A warm, salty fluid oozes over your face. It's blood!

You wonder if you have been wounded, but the only pain you feel is the crushing weight of the wolf upon your chest.

You slowly realize the beast no longer struggles. The wolf is dead! You wriggle from beneath the heavy body with great difficulty. Only then do you realize the creature landed on your sword as it leaped upon you!

The battle continues all around you. Baltek has slain three goblins, and Lydia is locked in fierce combat with the second wolf. The bats are darting and wheeling around Pentegarn. You can see only his staff swinging through the air.

Baltek kills the last goblin and rushes to aid the elf. With two powerful blows, he kills the snarling wolf.

Pale and shaken, Lydia sinks to the floor and says, "Thanks. I owe you one, fighter."

"Any time," Baltek says, then smiles shyly and adds, "for you."

The fighter strides toward Pentegarn, who is still overwhelmed by bats. Baltek disappears into the tangle of flying creatures. You see his sword flash once, then a clap of thunder and a puff of white smoke fill the room. When the smoke clears, Pentegarn stands unharmed, but Baltek lies motionless on the ground surrounded by the bats.

"Oh, no!" cries Lydia, rushing to the fighter's side. "You've killed him, Wizard."

"Don't worry, Lydia," the old man says. "We can fix him up in no time, if you'll help me drag him out of the way. We don't want to wake up any of these bats."

The three of you grasp his shoulders and pull the mighty fighter away from the bats. Pentegarn positions himself at the fighter's feet, then, pinching his eyes shut, he mutters some strange words and points his staff at Baltek. "That should do it."

But Baltek only begins to snore, making great deep rumbling sounds.

"You stupid old man," Lydia screeches. "How could you have been a great magician? You can't even undo your own spell!"

"Now dear, don't get upset," Pentegarn says. "It'll come to me in a moment."

He points his staff at Baltek and commands him to rise. Everyone stares hopefully at Baltek. There is silence...then another rumbling snore.

Pentegarn frowns at his failure, then raises his staff over his head in a final magical gesture. You cover your eyes, too scared to watch, and suddenly.

"Mmmmmm...I feel good!" says Baltek. "What's going on?"

"I knew you could do it, Pentegarn!" purrs Lydia.

"I got so sleepy all of a sudden!" Baltek continues. "What happened? Did I miss anything?"

"Never mind," Pentegarn snaps. "We should be on our way. Do we first go after the Ring of Spell Turning or the Cube of Mystic Forces?"

"Which is closest?" asks the elf.

"The ring," says the wizard. "But it's also the least powerful of the two."

"I think we should go for the ring," says Lydia. "Once we have it in our possession, it should help protect us against anything else we might meet."

"I myself would choose the cube, were the decision mine," says Owl.

"That's because you're such a square, beakbrain!" says Fox.

1. If you decide to seek the Ring of Spell Turning, go to page 137.
2. If you decide to seek the Cube of Mystic Forces, turn to page 50.

A soft night breeze filters down the tower stairway. Damp, clammy air, filled with the musty smell of dark cellars, drifts up from the dungeon stairs.

"I choose the tower!" you say.

"So be it," says Pentegarn. He turns upward.

You soon stand at the top of the stairs. The path to the tower lies before you. You slowly inch your way along the path, expecting a shriek of discovery at any moment. But nothing happens.

Pentegarn whispers, "The entrance is opposite us on the far side of the tower. It is quite probably guarded."

"Why don't I climb to the top of the tower?" whispers Lydia. "The top doesn't seem to be guarded. Then I can attach a rope, throw it down, and the rest of you can climb up. If we're lucky, maybe your staff is in the top half of the tower. If it's not, we can sneak down and attack from within."

"I think that's a good idea," you say.

"We can always hope!" says Pentegarn.

In the blink of an eye, Lydia darts away and starts climbing the tower. Even though you look directly at the tower, the elven thief is hard to see. She slips into every shadow as she creeps toward the top. You watch her progress breathlessly.

Lydia reaches the top and flashes you a quick smile before she disappears over the edge.

Long moments pass, and a cloud of bats burst forth. You hear nothing else, and no one appears at the tower's edge. Finally, just when you fear the worst, a rope flies down and dangles along the side of the tower. But Lydia does not appear.

Tucking Fox inside your shirt, you grasp the rope and start up. Pentegarn follows close behind, and Baltek brings up the rear, in case the old man tires or slips.

The climbing is hard, and the added weight of Fox does not help. Lydia made it look so easy! Your hands burn and ache with the strain, and the top of the tower seems very far away.

At last, your arms aching and your breath ragged from the climb, your hand feels the top of the tower and you call breathlessly, "Lydia, come help me, I'm so tired." There is no answer.

Straining to pull yourself up, you finally hook a leg over the wall. As you wait for your eyes to adjust to the darkness, you hear the familiar clacking of skeleton bones! You see an open treasure chest on the far side of the tower. Rubies, emeralds, diamonds, and pearls spill forth. You hear a clacking, and then Lydia, or what used to be Lydia, comes toward you...she's a skeleton! Her empty eye sockets stare at you. She grins horribly and holds out a bony hand.

Bracelets dangle from her wrist, and rings decorate her bony fingers. Necklaces of gold hang from her neck, and a crown of magnificent gems sits atop the glorious red hair which still crowns her empty skull. Although one hand extends toward you, the other is ready to strike with a dagger. The monster that was once your companion clacks slowly toward you.

Shaking with fear, you unhook your leg and, grasping the rope, scream, "Get Down! Hurry!"

Pentegarn and Baltek cannot know what you have seen, but they do not question the urgency in your voice. They climb down immediately, and you follow them down far more quickly than you rose. When you finally reach the end of your rope, you fall to the ground, gasping for breath.

As you lie on the ground, you see Lydia's skeleton climbing down the rope after you.

"Her greed was her downfall," says Pentegarn sadly. "It was a clever trap."

As you watch, huddled together in the tower's shadow, a thick black cloud pours from the tower. You hear the howling of wolves drawing close.

"That accursed skeleton is almost down the rope," growls Baltek. "And I don't like the look of that fog, or the sound of those wolves. I suggest we leave, now!"

"I concur," squawks Owl.

You retrace your steps as fast as you can. When you reach the mouth of the cavern, Baltek cries, "No good! Goblins! Run for the ledge!"

You don't want to venture along the narrow ledge, but you have no other choice. Reluctantly, you set out upon the tiny trail.

The first goblin sticks its head out of the cavern and screams excitedly, "Here they are! Hurry! Hurry!" You hear the gabble of goblin voices rushing up the trail. They will soon be upon you.

As the three of you edge along the ledge, the chill wind gusts violently, almost pulling you off the mountainside. The first of the goblins is nearing you. Its companions pour onto the trail, pushing and shoving each other in their excitement.

Baltek allows the goblin to draw near, then slams it with a powerful stroke. The goblin shrieks horribly and tumbles off the mountain. The remaining goblins hesitate, screaming with rage. Finally, their anger overcomes their fear and they rush after you.

"Run! Run for your lives!" Baltek screams, "I will hold them as long as I can!" He readies his sword for the advancing goblins.

You hate to leave him, but Pentegarn cannot travel the ledge alone. Besides, you would be of little or no use to Baltek. As the first goblins reach Baltek, you take Pentegarn's arm and hurry away along the ledge.

At last, Pentegarn stops. "We will wait here for Baltek."

At first, it seems Baltek will surely win as he slays goblin after goblin, but the tide of the battle slowly turns as he tires. Three goblins armed with pikes remain. They can stay out of Baltek's reach, yet still strike him easily. After tormenting Baltek for several minutes, one of the goblins finally knocks Baltek's sword from his hand. Moonlight shines on the blade as it tumbles end over end into the valley far below.

Baltek gives a chilling battle cry, and flings himself at the last three goblins! Trapping all three in his muscular arms, Baltek staggers, rolls, then falls from the ledge...and is gone forever.

"Baltek!" you scream, falling to your knees and peering over the edge. You see nothing of the brave fighter.

"Pentegarn, please do something magic!" you plead. "Bring Baltek back, please!"

"Even I cannot do that, Jaimie," the old man says sadly.

"First Lydia and now Baltek! It's too much, I can't bear it," you sob. "It's all over. We've lost!"

"We did our best," Owl says. "What more can we do?"

"Yeah, kid. Don't be so hard on yourself," says Fox. "You were great. Tree will be proud of you." Fox's voice quivers slightly.

Pentegarn wraps his thin arms about you and pats you on the back gently. "Owl and Fox are right. We did our best. Some of us gave all there is to give—our very lives. Death is never easy child, especially for those who are left behind. But you can bear it and you must do so. To do otherwise would mean Baltek gave his life in vain.

"Yet, the tale is not completely told, and perhaps hope shall grow from despair," Pentegarn says.

Your weeping slowly halts. "What do you mean, Pentegarn?"

"Have you never wondered why you are different from others your age? Why you can speak with animals and understand them? The answer is simple," Pentegarn says. "We share a rich and noble heritage, Jaimie, for you are my great grandchild. The blood of kings and queens flows in your veins. When I die, the rightful ownership of the staff will pass to you. But before that time arrives, we will have many years together to regain what the Evil One has stolen."

There is a moment of silence, and then Pentegarn says, "Come...come, child, we will go now. But I will teach you all I know. In time, we'll try again. And one day...ahh, yes, one day we will win!"

THE END

The pillar is very warm, indeed. Luckily, it does not burn your hands, and there are dozens of cracks to dig your fingers into.

You are nearly at the top when a tremendous shake loosens your grip and you slide ten feet back down the pillar. The stone is getting hot to the touch, and you are not sure you can hold on, but you know you must try.

Lydia screams from the top, "Help me! The pillar is crumbling and the ring is burning! We are doomed!"

"I'm not doomed," you say to yourself. Despite the fact that the pillar is starting to burn your hands, you give one last, great effort and scramble to the top.

Lydia stands on the pillar holding her hand in the air. Tears run down her cheeks as she peers at those below. You see the ring glowing brightly on her finger. It has a two-headed serpent entwined in holly leaves, with a large emerald set in the middle.

"Give me your hand," you say.

Lydia thrusts her hand at you. "It will do no good!" she screams, "I have tried to remove it."

"Someone else must remove it," Pentegarn calls, "someone innocent, as yet untouched by the trials of the world."

You quickly pull the ring from her finger. It is so hot you drop it as soon as you pull it from her finger.

The ring falls to the ground and lands at Pentegarn's feet.

"Thank you, young warrior," Lydia says. "You have saved my life."

The pillar no longer shakes, and its glow fades.

"Hey!" Fox cries. "Are you two staying up there all day? We're going to have company in a matter of minutes."

While you and Lydia scramble down the cracked pillar, Pentegarn places the ring on his finger. It comes to life as you touch the ground. The serpent slithers through the holly leaves and clings to his finger. The serpent's small eyes shine and its tiny mouths breathe little flames. The great stone shines with a life of its own.

"I thank you for saving both Lydia and the ring, Jaimie," Pentegarn says. "Were I certain you had the strength to wear it, I would give the ring to you in recognition of your great deed. But this is a very powerful and primitive thing, made from the very essences of good and evil. One must be not only pure, but strong of heart and wise of mind to wear it."

"You can keep the darn thing," Lydia says, rubbing her hand.

"Now we must seek the Cube of Mystic Forces," Pentegarn says. "We must watch

Please turn to next page.

carefully for monsters, for a pillar has moved. Surely, our enemy knows we are here."

Even as Pentegarn speaks, you see a change occurring in him. He is no longer old and bent-over; he is now a stately middle-aged man.

You gasp in wonder, and he says simply, "The ring has restored some of my power. We must seek the cube, if we wish to face the Evil One at full strength."

"I think not," says Baltek. "He knows we're down here now. He'll send his army of foul monsters down here to capture us. I like to fight, but I also like to live to fight again, so I say we go for the Evil One without the cube. Our chances are not good, I know, but if we try for the cube, we are certain to face hundreds of horrid creatures and never find the Evil One."

"I agree," says Lydia. "I've already faced one test. It nearly killed me, and everybody else along with me. I don't know what this Evil One is like, but he can't be any worse than the tests of the pillars. I say we sneak straight to the tower."

"What do you wish to do, Jaimie?" asks Pentegarn.

1. If you wish to try for the cube, turn to page 47.
2. If you wish to sneak straight to the tower, turn to page 53.

Thinking of all the scary things you have encountered so far—goblins, the skeleton patrol, the wolves,—you say, "If there's a chance we can sneak through with little or no danger, I'm for it. Let's go down."

Pentegarn sighs, "I never said the route was safe, but the die is cast. So be it."

Rising, he leads the way to the end of the ledge. Through the distant opening at the upper end of the staircase, you see a slice of white moon hanging on the night sky. On many nights, you have watched the same slice of moon through your bedroom window while lying safe and snug beneath your covers. Forcing your eyes away from the view, you turn and follow Pentegarn down into the dungeon.

You see nothing except a few bats. The air grows cold, damp, and musty, and Pentegarn's staff glows more dimly.

At last, the stairs end, and you find yourself in a passageway. You cannot see the end. Dripping water echoes everywhere, and your footing is slippery. You find it difficult to stand. Over the centuries, dripping water has formed stalactites and stalagmites everywhere. You feel as though you are walking through the teeth of a huge beast. Though you shudder with fear, you bravely control your fears.

You are ready to confess your fears when the narrow passage opens into a large cavern. A small hole opens to your left, about twenty feet away.

"I believe that is the secret passage to the tower I spoke of," Pentegarn says. "Some orcs attempting to invade my castle built it when I was younger."

Suddenly, you hear goblins raise a ferocious cry. "There they are! Catch them! Master want them!"

You now see a mob of goblins, perhaps fifty or more, running toward you out of the large cavern. You are certain you cannot defeat such a large number of them. The only question is which way do you run? Through the small opening to your right, or straight back up the stairs, into the night?

1. If you choose to run for the small opening, even though it is twenty feet from you, turn to page 56.
2. If you choose to run up the stairs, turn to page 75.

Even though it may well cost you your life, you must defend Pentegarn. With the mightiest battle-cry you can muster, you charge the giant skeleton.

The bony dragon-head lowers slowly as you run toward the creature's front legs. It opens its great mouth. Ignoring the impending doom, you swing your little sword at the dragon's shin. Amazingly, the sword bites into the bare bone and a tiny chip falls from the skeleton.

Fearing the bony mouth will seize you any second, you raise your sword to strike one last time before the end comes. Instead, though, a strong hand grasps your shoulder. Effortlessly, it pushes you back out of the way.

"Stay out of this, kid. Leave the fighting to me," says Baltek, swinging his mighty sword at the dragon's descending head. The head dodges Baltek's flashing sword, and Baltek uses the opportunity to swing at the skeleton's front leg.

"See kid? This is how you do it!" He completes his slash, and the skeleton's foot goes flying. He now rushes back and forth, slashing and swinging at the monster. The skeleton tries to follow Baltek, but it is slow, and Baltek is fast.

Another blow slices off part of the skeleton's tail. Zap! Baltek strikes the right shoulder, and pieces fly. The dragon tries to

Please turn to next page.

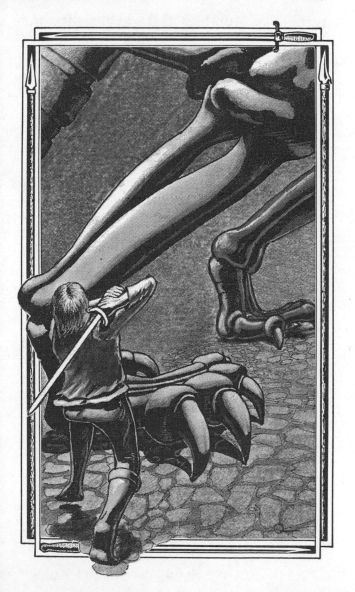

turn, but it stumbles as it wobbles after the mighty warrior. The great neck extends forward for just a moment. Crunch! Baltek's sword bashes down on the neck. The blow slices through the neck and soon the awful creature lies shattered and still.

You edge around the skeleton and reach Baltek's side.

"See kid?" breathes Baltek. "You've got to learn to pick your fights. Never get into a fight you can't win, unless the stakes are so great you are willing to die."

"They were," you say, glancing shyly at Pentegarn.

Pentegarn drapes a thin arm around your shoulder. "I thank you, my young friend."

Baltek eyes you thoughtfully. "Anyway," he says, "you held it off long enough for me to get there. You'll be a mighty warrior in a few years."

"Baltek," Pentegarn says, "we thank you for disposing of the Guardian of the Cube. And I thank you, Jaimie, for saving me from what would have been a most uncomfortable end.

"When you are rested and ready, Baltek," Pentegarn continues, "we shall try for the cube."

"I was born ready!" answers Baltek. "There's no need to wait. That was merely a warm-up exercise."

"All right, but I warn you," says Pente-garn. "This is no easy task. Even if we are lucky enough to get the cube, there will be no time to rest. We will have to flee as though our lives depended on it, as indeed they will."

Baltek removes his sweat-slickened armor and flexes his arm and leg muscles. His body is covered with a film of sweat. Never have you seen such enormous muscles.

With a fierce look on his face, the muscular fighter approaches the shiny cornerstone. He studies it for a long moment, then bends down and digs his fingers under its base. He closes his eyes and lifts. Sweat breaks out upon his forehead and pours down his face. Every muscle in his body is stretched to its limit and beyond.

The stone does not move at first, then you hear a deep groan. The fighter's face grows deep red. A terrible grimace of pain and exhaustion creases his brow. He is near the end of his powers, but still he strains against the the great weight.

You hear a screech, like the earth ripping apart, and the enormous cornerstone moves. Lydia tries to sneak her hand under the stone to pull the cube away.

"Higher, Baltek!" she cries.

Even straining with all his might, the fighter cannot raise the stone any higher. Again she tries to snake her hand under the pillar.

"Just a little higher," she cries, "I can feel it beneath my fingers."

But Baltek only groans, and the pillar slips a fraction of an inch down. Lydia jerks her hand from beneath the pillar.

"If only my hand were smaller!"

Baltek groans again, and nearly drops the stone as he loses his grip. Luckily, however, his fingers catch on the side of the stone and he stops it before it drops to the ground.

"Hurry," he gasps, "I can't hold!"

The pillar slips yet again, and Pentegarn says, "We must succeed, Baltek! Without the cube, we cannot defeat the Evil One. You must move the pillar!"

Baltek closes his eyes, then groans mightily. The pillar rises a fraction of an inch, and Baltek appears to tire. But, instead of dropping the pillar, Baltek holds it for a moment, straining against the great weight. His face grows red, and the veins in his neck stick out. The strain disappears from his face for moment.

Baltek suddenly yells, lifts, and heaves with his last ounce of strength. The pillar moves three feet to the right, and Baltek lets it crash to the ground.

You see a great depression in the earth where the pillar stood, and in it the cube lies nearly buried. It is plain and ordinary; you see nothing to indicate it has any magical powers.

Please, turn to next page.

In spite of his insistence on speed, Pentegarn moves toward the cornerstone as though in a daze. You shake his elbow gently.

"Pentegarn," you say. "What's wrong with you? Are you still with us?"

"What?" He blinks, noticing you at last. "Oh yes, my child. It's nothing, nothing. Nothing at all." The light returns to his eyes. "Despite my efforts over all these long years, I never believed I would hold the Cube of Mystic Forces in my hands again."

"But why did you keep trying if you believed it could not be done?" you ask.

"Because when you want something more than life itself, your want overshadows everything else. Though I did not believe I could retrieve the cube, I had to try!" He falls silent for a long moment.

"Come on, Pentegarn," you finally say. "We can't waste any time. The stone's been moved."

"Yes, child. You're right, of course!" Pentegarn agrees.

He stoops and takes the cube into his hand. Pentegarn holds the cube on the flat of his hand, presses it in two places, and a dazzling light—nearly as bright as the sun—bursts forth.

Raising your hands to your eyes, you peer through your fingers. Pentegarn stands at the heart of the brilliant light, seemingly

Please turn to next page.

unaffected. The cube sends forth its throbbing ray even more brightly. You cover your face completely and turn to the wall, unable to bear its intensity.

At long last, the light dims. You carefully lower your arms and turn around. Your hands drop to your sides and your mouth falls open. Pentegarn is gone!

A healthy, middle-aged man almost as tall as Baltek stands in his place. He holds the cube on the flat of his palm, as Pentegarn did moments earlier. Now the cube merely sparkles and twinkles like a giant diamond.

"Where is Pentegarn?" you cry angrily, raising your sword.

The tall figure bursts into laughter. "Jaimie, put your sword down. It is I, Pentegarn."

"How can it be?" you cry.

"The cube, little one," he answers, "the cube. Its force has returned some of the power and strength stripped from me by the loss of my staff."

"Whatever the cause, I'm glad!" says Baltek. There is a bounce to the warrior's step, and he seems untouched by his great effort. "It usually takes me a while to recover from pulls like that, but I feel fine! As long as we're all here and ready, I suggest we leave before the monsters get here."

136

"Yes, indeed," Pentegarn says. "Come, my friends. Now we must retrieve the ring."

You can scarcely take your eyes off the kingly figure striding so strongly before you. It is evident the others feel the same, for expressions are cheerful and full of hope. Even Fox has nothing bad to say!

You are trying hard to keep up with Pentegarn when he halts abruptly.

"Our first encounter," Pentegarn says. "This should be fun!"

"Speak for yourself, king," says Lydia quickly, "I don't like the odds. I say we find another way to the ring."

You peer around Pentegarn's robes and see a great mob of goblins pouring down the corridor toward you!

"Let me at 'em," growls Baltek. "We may not win, but there won't be many of them standing when I'm through."

The decision is yours. Should you try to outrun the angry mob of goblins and find a safe place to hide? Or should you try to defeat the horde of goblins?

1. If you choose to run, turn to page 56.
2. If you want to rely on your luck and Baltek's strength and skill, turn to page 146.

"Let's try for the ring," you say.

"The ring lies just ahead!" says Pentegarn. "Let us continue." Your small band hurries along the corridor, watching all directons for enemies.

At last, Pentegarn leads you into a huge cavern with a tall black pillar rising from a massive cornerstone. Both the cornerstone and the pillar are made of some type of polished stone. The pillar soars upward, disappearing into the gloom above.

Pentegarn turns to Lydia. "You will have to climb the pillar and retrieve the ring, my dear. You must set aside all thief-like thoughts and concentrate on the good of the party. If you cannot do so, it will bring disaster down upon all of us."

"What are you trying to pull?" screams Lydia. "When you came to the Salty Dog Inn, you wanted a low-down, sneaky thief who knew the dirtiest tricks of the trade! That's who you got, me! What's all this goody-two-shoes stuff?"

"Quite true," says the old man. "But the ring's safeguard is purity. The person who handles it must be entirely pure and free from evil thoughts, or it will mean their death. So, you see, you must perform your greatest trick of all, and pretend to be good!"

"I'll do it on one condition," says Lydia. "You must promise me you'll never tell anyone I did this. It could ruin my reputation!"

"Don't worry, we won't breathe a word," Pentegarn says. "Now climb that pillar and think good thoughts!"

The elf wipes her hands on her pants and scrambles up the cornerstone.

"This is slippery," she says. "It's not going to be easy."

You gather in a tight bunch at the foot of the cornerstone, watching in suspense as Lydia slowly inches her way up the slippery pillar. For every foot she gains, she slips back three or four inches. She climbs slowly...so very slowly, but she continues to make progress. She's almost to the top—she's going to make it! A mightly groan escapes her lips, and she slips halfway down the pillar.

You hear Lydia muttering to herself as she scrambles back up the pillar. Finally, she fights her way to the top. "I'm here!" she yells. "This ring had better be worth all this trouble." She disappears from view for several seconds.

"Wow! This is really nice," she yells. "You didn't tell me it would be so pretty. It's covered with jewels. I wonder if it will fit me."

"No, Lydia!" cries Pentegarn. "Don't put it on. Toss it down to me! It's too powerful for you!"

"You're just saying that because you don't want to share it with me! You can't imagine how beautiful it is on my finger. This big emerald is the same color as my eyes."

Lydia sits down and admires the ring.

"We must stop her," Pentegarn says. "We must get the ring from her, or she will destroy herself."

"How?" asks Baltek. "I can't climb that slick pillar."

"Were it not for my impaired wing," Owl says, "I would fly up and pluck the object from her hand."

"Jaimie," Pentegarn says, "you are our only hope. You must climb the pillar and take the ring from her finger."

"It won't be an easy job, kid," says Baltek. "She is an experienced infighter, and she's twice as cunning as any elf I've ever met."

A horrified wail floats down from the pillar. Lydia screeches, "What have I done? The ring is burning my finger!"

"It's too late," cries Pentegarn, sinking to his knees. "You have failed us, Lydia. All is lost. Come down, we must flee or die."

"I can't. The ring is too hot, I can't use my hand," she cries. "Help me!"

The pillar has started to tremble. You feel warmth flooding from it.

"If you're going to rescue her, kid," Baltek says. "You've got to do it now."

"There's no use," Pentegarn says. "You could never climb the pillar in time to remove the ring from her finger. Soon, the whole pillar will crash down around us; we would only be wasting more lives by asking anybody to climb the pillar."

Are you going to climb the pillar and remove the ring from Lydia's finger?

1. If the answer is yes, turn to page 123.
2. If you agree you cannot climb the pillar in time, turn to page 150.

You descend into darkness.

"Is it possible no one is here?" you ask.

"It is not!" a deep voice whispers.

A brilliant silvery light suddenly floods the room. Shielding your eyes, you see that the light springs from a weathered staff of great age. But the light is so dazzling you cannot see who—or what—holds it.

"Who dares hold the Staff of Kings, the staff of Pentegarn?" cries Pentegarn.

A low chuckle fills the room. "Don't you know me, Pentegarn? We've met often enough."

The light dims to a soft glow. You can now see everything in the room. Dozens of skeletons and goblins, all armed and snarling, stand along the walls. The staff stands in the center of the room, glowing softly. An ugly, thick black cloud billows about its base.

As you watch, the cloud pulses and throbs as though alive. It suddenly mushrooms to enormous size, and, before your astonished eyes, turns into a vast horde of shrilling, chittering bats! The foul, hot stink of their bodies fills your breath. You strike out wildly at the furry creatures, but they avoid your blows. Lydia screams, "Bats! I hate bats! Get them out of here!"

Just as you think you will surely go mad, the bats disappear, replaced by the swirling black fog. Gasping with fear, you draw closer together.

The black fog spins like a small cyclone beside the staff and then disappears. In its place stands an enormous black wolf with fire-red eyes and long white fangs. It crouches, snarling and whining. Its back legs bunch, and it springs at you! You throw up your arms to protect yourself, but the wolf disappears in mid-leap and the black fog returns.

Please turn to next page.

Once more it begins to churn, changing shape and size with every breath. It moves back to the staff. Slowly, a bent black figure, covered head to toe by a dark cloak, appears. You cannot see its face, only a bit of the swirling black fog—more terrifying than any face could possibly be. It keeps its hands tucked inside the folds of its sleeves.

"As you can see," says the Evil One's hollow voice, "I have many faces. I am darkness. I am fear. I am your nightmares." The chilling voice pauses, then continues, "Bow down and pay homage to my power!"

"No!" cries Pentegarn. "Not so long as I live!" Raising his young staff, a mere twig compared to the Staff of Kings, he points it at the black figure.

A shaft of lightning blasts out of the end of the staff toward the enemy. The Dark One raises its hand and points its own staff at Pentegarn. The bolt stops in mid-air, quivers, and retraces its passage. As the bolt hits the young staff, a clap of thunder fills the room, and the small staff bursts, falling to the ground in a million smoking shards.

"Do not try petty tricks on me," the voice sneers. "How dare you challenge me when I have this?"

He raises the staff, and holds it in front of himself. Pentegarn steps toward the staff, and the goblins step forward menacingly, their weapons raised.

"Bow to my power or die!" the figure hisses as the goblins approach.

1. Are you going to bow to its power, hoping to buy more time? If so, turn to page 93.
2. Or are you going to fling yourself at the staff, hoping you can surprise the Evil One and knock the staff from its grasp? Turn to page 68.

Hoping you have made the correct decision, you draw your sword and take your place beside Baltek.

Pentegarn steps in front of you and moves his hand over the cube. The goblins continue to advance steadily. You almost step in front of Pentegarn to protect him from the goblins, but Baltek holds your shoulder.

"He's got something up his sleeve, Jaimie," the fighter says.

Pentegarn raises the cube, mumbling magic words. The goblins, almost within striking range, continue to advance. They scream, "Get them! Master want them!"

The cube flashes, then glows brightly. Still clutching your sword, you raise an arm to cover your face. You close your eyes against the glare.

"Help!" the goblins scream. "Run away. Run away!" Peeking from under your arm, you see the goblins running down the corridor in the nearly blinding light. Knowing how hard it is for you to see, you can imagine how painful the light must have been for the foul goblins, who love only dark places.

You hurry along the corridor into another cavern. Like the one that held the cube, a large pillar rises high into the air from a huge cornerstone.

"Wait for me, friends," Pentegarn says. "I'll be right back."

He closes his eyes, gripping his staff with one hand and the cube with the other, then utters a mysterious word and zooms into the air!

When he reaches the top of the pillar, he lands and quickly picks the ring off of it. He flies back toward you.

As Pentegarn lands, he says, "There, that didn't take long. I've forgotten how much fun flying can be. I shall have to do it more often!"

Pentegarn holds the ring out for you to see. It's incredible! It looks like a circlet of holly leaves fashioned from heavy gold. Small diamonds, rubies, and emeralds are sprinkled upon the leaves. A silver two-headed serpent lies coiled about a large gem in the center. The amazing stone flashes silver, green, blue, and red in the light.

Pentegarn places the ring on his right hand. The serpent slithers through the holly leaves and clings to Pentegarn's finger! Small eyes open and tiny mouths breathe flames. The great stone gleams with a life all its own.

"This is a very powerful and primitive thing," Pentegarn says. "It is made from the very essence of good and evil. You must be very strong, indeed, to bear it."

You stare in fascination. When you look up at last, Pentegarn stands straight and tall, a man in the prime of his life. He is as big as Baltek, and his hair is now a rich, shiny brown.

"My lord," you say, bowing.

"This is no time for ceremony, Jaimie. There is still much to be done. We must face the Evil One himself. We now begin the most hazardous portion of our trial, and the risk is severe, indeed."

Without further comment, Pentegarn turns and leads the way down a dark, foul-smelling corridor.

Turn to page 58.

You stare at the pillar, now casting a bright white glow. The glow becomes more intense, and deepens to light rose color as you approach.

"Come," says Pentegarn. "We must leave while there is still time. All is lost. Our only hope is to leave and try again."

But you cannot move. The sight of the pillar is too compelling.

"Help!" screams Lydia. "Save me!"

"We cannot," cries Pentegarn. "You have let greed and vanity overcome you!"

"I'm not scared, I'll help her!" says Baltek. Pushing you aside, he scrambles up the cornerstone.

"Baltek, come back! It's hopeless!" calls Pentegarn. Baltek ignores the cries and begins to inch his way up the pillar.

Baltek is a third of the way up the pillar, fighting for every small gain. Suddenly, the column changes color once again and turns pale red. Hairline cracks appear, and a deep rumble sounds all around you.

Baltek cries out, "I cannot do it!" and falls back upon the cornerstone.

Lydia screams long and horribly. The pillar rocks back and forth, glowing bright red. The cracks are now very large. All at once, an enormous rumble comes from the pillar. It cracks into four pieces and the sections begin to move apart.

The floor at your feet shifts sideways, then tilts up before you. You and Pentegarn are thrown down.

Lydia gives a heart-stopping screech, and the entire pillar breaks apart and crashes to the ground. An avalanche of earth and stone pours from the ceiling. The roar of earth and stone colliding deafens you.

A slab of upturned stone offers a tiny nook of safety, and you all duck beneath its protection.

Boulders and hot glowing chunks of the pillar bounce past you. After several long minutes, the avalanche of rock stops and you dare to look around.

The entire area is filled with glowing, burning rock. You see no sign of Baltek or Lydia. You stare in grief at your companions' grave and tears come to your eyes.

"Pentegarn," you cry. "We failed. All is lost!"

"You're right in one sense, Jaimie," Pentegarn says heavily. "There is no hope for the mission now. We will have to retreat. But all is not lost, for I have a secret to tell you which may allow us to return someday and snatch victory from the jaws of defeat. The blood of kings and queens flows in your veins, Jaimie, for you are my great grandchild. We may have failed in this attempt, but we will return together, if you will, and challenge the Evil One once again!"

Although deadly danger surrounds you, you feel as though a great weight has been lifted from your shoulders. You now understand the reason you have always felt different. You now know why you feel so close to this old man, and why you felt compelled to help him!

You hug Pentegarn tightly. A warm glow of happiness spreads over his face, and he rises to leave. Slowly, you travel through the tunnels and cautiously make your way into the secret room under the stairs. Soon, you are outside in the cool, clean night air.

"How good it is to smell the fresh air outside that evil abode!" Owl says.

"Speak for yourself, birdbrain," Fox says, "I won't be happy until we're safe and sound under Tree's branches."

"We'll return," Pentegarn says weakly, "I'll teach you all I know. Jaimie, where's my staff? How far is it to your village? I'm tired. So very tired. But once I rest, I'll be fine."

Your heart sinks. You are not at all certain he will ever be fine again. But as long as there is hope, you will stand by him.

THE END

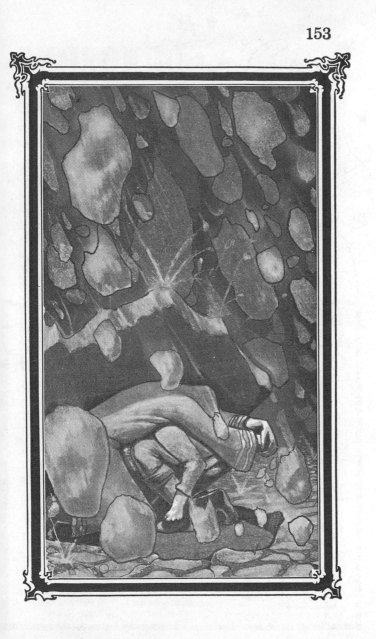

DUNGEONS & DRAGONS® BASIC SET

DUNGEONS & DRAGONS™ ENDLESS QUEST™ Books

"PILLARS OF PENTEGARN"

A wizard, a fighter, a crafty elf maiden, and **you**, the reader, must fight the evil Master to save a kingdom. **Your** decisions may lead **you** to the ruins of Castle Pentegarn, encounters with scary monsters, and the incredible Staff of Kings.

"MOUNTAIN OF MIRRORS"

Why have the vital supply caravans failed to reach **your** village? The village elders have sent **you**, a young elf, to the Mountain of Mirrors to solve the mystery. Can **you** return to warn the village of things **you** discover before it is too late?

"DUNGEON OF DREAD"

An evil wizard has been using his dark powers to harm and enslave others. With the aid of Laurus, a timid halfling, **you** must travel through the dangerous caverns and tunnels of the wizard's mountain to find and challenge him.

"RETURN TO BROOKMERE"

You are sole heir to the elven throne. The ancestral castle, however, was seized long ago by vast armies of goblins and orcs. **You** must return there to find what force holds the castle against the elves.